The Healing Garden

It is better to write books than to plant vines.
The latter gratifies the stomach, the former the soul.

Alcuin of York, 735 AD

The Healing Garden

Michael Bailes
The Fragrant Garden, Erina, Australia

Kangaroo Press

First published in 1994 by Kangaroo Press Pty Ltd
3 Whitehall Road Kenthurst NSW 2156 Australia
P.O. Box 6125 Dural Delivery Centre NSW 2158
Typeset by G.T. Setters Pty Limited
Printed by Southwood Press, Marrickville 2204

ISBN 0 86417 636 8

Contents

To my wife Jan,
who introduced me to plants—
and proofreading.

Introduction

Be careful about reading health books.
You may die of a misprint.

Mark Twain

I have tried to make this, my collection of remedies, as practical, as useful and as simple as possible. Most plants mentioned are readily available and easy to grow in a small herb garden. Otherwise, a quick trip to the kitchen, supermarket or health food shop will find the plants and herbs I mention. Unusual or hard-to-find herbs are only included if they have some exceptional effect on a particular complaint.

I have not tried to cover all complaints or all remedies. I have grown all the herbs and tried many of the remedies myself; others I have (fortunately) not had reason to try.

Loving the old herbals, I have included many quotes from them. I am also interested in modern medicinal research. For a twentieth century reader, both old herbalist and modern scientist can be equally difficult to understand: the scientist has his specialised scientific language and research techniques; the old herbalists have their archaic language and olde world view. However, these quotes are not essential for you to use and understand this book. I like them because I find it fascinating to see that the modern scientist and the ancient herbalist often say the same thing. This I find a cause of joy and wonder.

Because I believe that humour is the best medicine, I have approached the topic of health in a light-hearted (but not frivolous) way. When I worked in a psychiatric hospital you could always tell the sane people—they were the ones with the sense of humour. Humour is, in itself, healing. Watching a funny video or film is a healing act.

Humour puts everything into perspective and stops us taking ourselves too seriously. It was very hard to find much fun in any of the books on medicine or medicinal herbs in my library. This, in itself, is a sad commentary on the state of medicinal writing.

Disease and sickness are defined, created and cured by the society in which we live and they reflect that society's values and attitudes. I have thus found myself spending some time and space on the immune system, the heart and circulatory disorders. I would not think this necessary if I belonged to a less affluent culture. I often wonder how different this book would have been if I lived in Africa and the problem was where the next meal was coming from, rather than how much animal fat it contained.

What we accept as 'cures' often says more about our attitudes and values and the belief system of our society than it says about science or herbalism. Healing is a journey, not necessarily a cure. Although this book is divided into sections on specific complaints, these are only the starting points of your journey. The ritual of growing, preparing and using your own herbs is in itself healing. It means *you* have made a decision to get well. Let your mind and the herbs work together.

If you have a favourite remedy you think I have neglected, drop me a line. I may be able to include it in a future edition of the book and it could improve someone's day!

Michael Bailes
The Fragrant Garden 1994

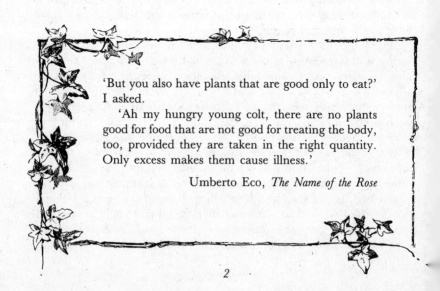

'But you also have plants that are good only to eat?' I asked.

'Ah my hungry young colt, there are no plants good for food that are not good for treating the body, too, provided they are taken in the right quantity. Only excess makes them cause illness.'

Umberto Eco, *The Name of the Rose*

The Healing Garden

Our bodies are our gardens, to which our wills are gardeners; so that if we plant nettles or sow lettuce, set hyssop and weed up thyme, supply it with one gender of herbs or distract it with many ... why the power and corrigible authority of this lies in our wills

Shakespeare *Othello* Act I, Scene III.

The Healing Garden should contain simple, safe and inexpensive fresh herbs, many of which you may already use in your cooking. Your medicine garden should also contain ingredients for a few lotions and potions. These you can make from fresh herbs or you can purchase them ready made from chemists or health food shops.

Remember that the Chinese use herbs in their daily diet to maintain their health. They use simple remedies such as cabbage, garlic, ginger and sesame. We tend to view medicine as something much more dramatic, such as antibiotics, sleeping tablets and pain killers. Few Westerners would see their breakfast and lunch as medicine. I aim to show how simple kitchen herbs can be used to aid a whole range of common medical complaints.

Many herbalists believe that the human digestive system has the ability to take from the complex chemistry of plants just what is needed and to discard the rest. For example, if you take a lot of vitamin B, the excess is excreted (very brightly) in the urine. By providing a varied diet of herbs and vegetables we are giving the body a smorgasbord of chemicals to use as medicine. Including a variety of green plants in your diet is, therefore, good medicine.

Your Healing Garden

Main herbs to grow

Aloe vera, lemon balm, celandine, sage, lemon thyme, feverfew, yarrow, mugwort, chilli, peppermint, German camomile, echinacea.

Some others (mentioned for one or two specific complaints)

Southernwood, borage, rosemary, meadowsweet, wood betony, liquorice (only if keen—easier to buy), parsley, mint.

Medicinal vegetables and fruit

Onion, ginger, garlic, potato, lemon, carrot, cabbage.

Other kitchen medicines

Sesame seed, salt, vinegar, tea (green and black), chilli sauce.

Healing from the wine cellar

Wine, brandy, gin, bitters.

Basic Herbal First Aid Cabinet

These herbs will make up the bare bones of your healing cabinet. Specific health problems might then call for other herbs. Some herbs, like Golden Seal, may need to be purchased from a herbal chemist because they are difficult to grow in most parts of Australia.

Ointments

Comfrey, Golden Seal, arnica, calendula, tea tree

Essential Oils

Lavender, tea tree, rosemary, camomile, sandalwood or cedarwood and The Fragrant Garden Breathe Easy Oil. As these are highly concentrated, they should be purchased.

Dried Herbs

These can be grown or purchased: green and black tea, camomile tea, peppermint tea.
These should be purchased: slippery elm powder, ginseng.

> If the body doesn't betray you with a sudden failure such as a myocardial infarction, chemicals and radiation are sure to give you cancer. If degenerative arthritis or herpes doesn't afflict you, you are likely to sprain your ankle, or fall prey to lacerations. The world is full not only of bacteria and poisons, but of sharp objects and hard places to fall. No matter what you do to stay healthy, you are likely to fail. Hypochondriacs know that the world is an incredibly dangerous place and are surprised—and rightly so—to be alive at all. They expect to be sick. Their only question is: 'What is wrong with me today?'
>
> James Gorman, *First Aid For Hypochondriacs*

Acne

I once had a very cranky lady wander into the nursery and pointedly ask, 'Are they the biggest Aloe vera plants you have?' I swiftly dragged the biggest aloe I could find up the hill from our propagation area. Delighted, she told me why she'd needed such large plants. She used aloe daily, as a face cream. As she had oily skin the aloe was ideal, and she found it the best and cheapest form of cosmetic cream. Now, alas, her two teenage daughters had also discovered that it cured their acne and had proceeded to massacre her carefully tended plant.

Fresh aloe leaf alleviates acne in three ways. Firstly, it is astringent and helps dry out the pimples and blackheads. Secondly, it is antiseptic and reduces bacterial problems. Thirdly, aloe contains allantoin and germanium which encourage and promote the body's own repair system; damaged skin repairs itself faster when aloe is applied. To use the aloe, break open a 5 cm square and rub in the clear, soothing gel. Many people expect it to be sticky but are amazed how it quickly soothes and penetrates the skin, leaving a silky softness. Although the yellow sap underneath the skin is also medicinal, it does stain, so try not to get it on your clothes.

A diet high in protein, low in sugars and low in concentrated carbohydrates (i.e. sugary soft drinks, lollies and cakes) is often helpful. So too is a diet low in dairy products, fatty foods and foods containing iodine (e.g. seaweed and salt, to which iodine is usually added). Vitamin and mineral supplements such as vitamins A, E, C, zinc, chromium and selenium can also be helpful. (Selenium is only available on prescription in Australia but is freely available in other countries. There is some contention about which form is most easily absorbed.)

Marigold flowers or calendula, pressed between the fingers and applied morning and night directly to pimples, is also safe and effective. Make sure your hands are clean.

Adrenal Gland Tonic

The adrenal glands are probably one of our most important and most abused glands. They bear the brunt of twentieth century stresses. Poor adrenal gland function can cause such problems as depression, mood changes and hypoglycaemia (low blood sugar).[1] Some of the herbs that seem to help the adrenal glands are borage, liquorice and ginseng. The Chinese consider ginseng and liquorice their two greatest herbs.

Borage

Borage is an attractive, easily grown annual herb, with pretty star-shaped blue flowers. Its hairy leaves have a pleasant cucumber flavour. Include some young leaves and flowers, freshly picked, in your salad. Rub the leaves between two tea towels to remove the hairiness if you find it unpleasant. Borage was traditionally added to alcoholic drinks such as Pimms. It is possible that the alcohol makes some of the minerals in borage more easily absorbed. Borage can also be taken as a tea, or a tincture can be bought from health food stores.

Liquorice

An amazing medicinal plant, but don't confuse the herb liquorice with the lolly. Most liquorice confectionery is made with man-made anise flavour. You can buy real liquorice lollies, but you have to search for them. You can also buy the pure liquorice juice in a solid stick, a wonderfully strong flavour but an acquired taste!

Ginseng

Like borage and liquorice, ginseng is what the Chinese herbalists call an adaptogen—something that helps the body to cope. Ginseng is best taken as a tea. You should avoid taking caffeine-containing drinks such as coffee at the same time as ginseng tea, because the ginseng enhances the stimulating effects of the caffeine. Recent research has shown that many of these adaptogenic herbs contain the chemical germanium, of which the scientists say:

> The apparent versatility of Ge–132 [a form of germanium] normalises homeostasis, stimulates immunity and alleviates major diseases, all of which suggest that it acts at a fundamental level of life function.[2]

Translated, that means that the herbs containing germanium can keep us healthy and prevent us getting sick.

Other rare herbs that Japanese researchers have found to encourage adrenal hormone production include *Bupleurum falcatum* (Hare's ear), *Camellia sinensis* (tea, the ordinary variety found in every supermarket), *Styrax japonicus* (Japanese snowbell), *Polygala senega* (seneca snakeroot), *Sapindus mukorossi* (Chinese soapberry), *Gypsophyla paniculata* (Baby's breath), *Aesculus hippocastanum* (European horsechestnut) and *Platycodon grandiflorum* (Balloon flower).

Allergies

Food Allergies

Food allergies are one of the most insidious of all disorders and one unfortunately ignored by many general practitioners. In contrast, alternative practitioners see allergy as the source of almost all disease. Symptoms of food allergy can include intense tiredness followed by periods of restlessness, hyperactivity or sleeplessness; irritability; depression; muscle weakness; cravings for foods, drugs, sweets or alcohol; low blood sugar (hypoglycaemia); aches and pains; headaches; malaise; skin rashes; dandruff; aggressive behaviour and 'foggy brain' (the inability to think clearly). Many GPs pass these symptoms off as stress or hypochondria. Treatment of stress can help allergies because stress can aggravate them.

We can have an allergy to almost any food, not just to 'junk' food. Healthy treats such as oranges, tomatoes, milk, fish, eggs and bread can often be a cause. Reactions are always very individual. More often, however, preservatives such as sulphur, flavour enhancers such as monosodium glutamate (MSG), and food colourings such as 'sunset yellow' can trigger allergic reactions.

Robert Buist, editor of *International Clinical Nutrition Review*, has written a number of helpful books on the subject of allergies—they are probably the best in their field.[3,4]

A simple emergency remedy for mild to moderate food allergies (severe ones can result in anaphylaxis and death if not treated medically) is to take a half to one teaspoon of bicarbonate of soda in water. If this is not available, drink lots of soda water. Digestive bitters are sometimes helpful. Most health food shops have a large range of these.

The herb Pau d'arco *(Tabebuia heptaphylla)* has also been getting a little attention of late for its usefulness with allergies. Adrenal gland and liver tonics can also be helpful.

Allergies are an immune system disorder and immune system support should be given *(see Immune System)*.

Antibiotics

Garlic

Garlic is about 1% as strong an antibiotic as penicillin. But the potency of garlic is such that about 1 mg of garlic is equivalent to 15 Oxford units of penicillin. Thus a large clove of garlic is roughly equal to one 250 mg penicillin capsule.[5]

Garlic can be eaten as a vegetable. Peel 50 or more cloves, place in water and bring the water to the boil, change the water and bring to the boil again. Change the water once more. Changing the water makes the flavour milder, so you decide how many times you want to do this. For me twice is enough. Every time you change the water you will lose some of the garlic's potency. The garlic cloves, so treated, taste like mildly garlic-flavoured beans. Toss the cloves in a little butter before serving. While boiling might destroy some of the medicinal effect of the garlic, you can eat a lot of garlic painlessly this way. The next day your fragrance is astounding, but you won't have a cold.

You can buy garlic tablets from the health food store, or just make your own by slicing cloves into pill-sized portions! This is cheaper and often more effective than tablets. Many southern Europeans eat fresh garlic like apples.

Essential Oils

Other antibiotics include most essential oils, which are very strong bactericides. To combat an external ear canal infection, for example, warm an egg-cup full of olive oil and place up to 10 drops of lavender oil in it. Place a few drops of the still warm mixture in the ear *(see Ears)*.

Cone Flower *(Echinacea purpurea)*

Echinacea is a pretty garden flower sometimes called Blackeyed Susan, but do not confuse it with the myriad backyard plants that go by this common name. It is easy to grow in a sunny, well drained spot. The stringy roots are traditionally boiled and made into a tea for all sorts of complaints. Recently research has shown the plant stimulates the body's own defence system against invading bugs *(see Immune System)*. It seems safe to use for children and adults.

Antiseptics

All essential oils are antiseptic; they do vary a little in their relative strength. A few drops of lavender essential oil or tea tree oil to a cup of water is a good all-purpose antiseptic for cuts and scratches.

Aphrodisiacs

> Half past nine—high time for supper;
> 'Cocoa, love?' 'Of course, my dear.'
> Helen thinks it quite delicious,
> John prefers it now to beer,
> Knocking back the sepia potion,
> Hubby winks, says, 'Who's for bed?'
> 'Shan't be long,' says Helen softly,
> Cheeks a faintly flushing red.
>
> Stanley J. Sharpless, 'Cupid's Nightcap'

Chocolate has a reputation as an aphrodisiac. It contains the stimulants caffeine, theobromine and phenylethylamine. Montezuma, said to have had a harem of 600, drank 50 cups of chocolate a day.

Ginseng is the safest and most readily available aphrodisiac herb, especially for men. Ginseng is a general tonic that helps normalise blood pressure. As failure to produce an erection can be caused by circulatory

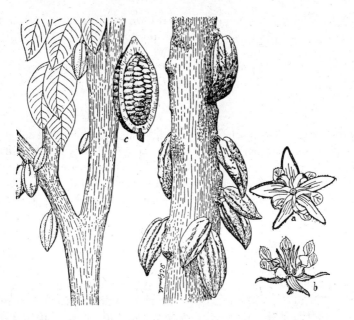

problems, ginseng may help; it has a tonic effect on the whole circulatory system.

Ginseng instant tea sachets are available. If you don't like the flavour (it tastes a little like mud) mix it with your martinis or gin! Take about 10 g a day for four or five weeks. Do not take it with drinks containing caffeine as this might cause insomnia and is not good for your liver. (The ginseng potentiates the effects of caffeine.)

Rosemary essential oil stimulates blood supply. A few drops can be added to the bath. A massage oil or bath with essential oil of sandalwood can also be helpful.

It is important for men to have adequate zinc in their diet to maintain a healthy sperm count. Oysters, the traditional food for lovers, contain very large amounts of zinc. In fact, they are one of the richest sources of zinc. About six raw oysters have 60 mg zinc, compared with only 3 mg in the same amount of beef liver, another concentrated source. Normal men with zinc deficiencies do not produce enough testosterone and sperm, and can become infertile or impotent. Other foods high in zinc include crab, lobster, lean beef, brown rice, lean pork, salmon and fish.

Fish and seafood are traditionally said to be helpful aphrodisiacs. Perhaps this is because of their high zinc content. We know that fish can reduce blood cholesterol (if not deep fried!). Good blood supply is important for male sexual performance, so...

Old impotent Alden from Walden
Ate salmon to heat him to scaldin'
'Twas just the ticket
To stiffen his wicket
This salmon of Amorous Alden.

Anon

Some interesting South American herbs, if you can find them, are damiana, saw palmetto, yohimbe and muira-puama. Most of these have some effect, but they should only be taken under medical supervision. Here is an interesting recipe from a Canadian herbalist magazine,[6] although it may just be a sure way to ruin a good bottle of whisky!

Damiana Liqueur

Soak 30 g damiana leaves, two tablespoons of saw palmetto berries, two tablespoons angelica root and ½ tablespoon of vanilla pods in 750 ml whisky. After one week, strain the mixture through a coffee filter and save the liquid. Resoak the herbs, etc, in 750 ml of distilled water for another week and then strain this second mixture. Heat the second mixture to approximately 80°C and dissolve one cup of honey into the hot liquid. After the honey has dissolved, remove from heat, allow to cool somewhat and then add it to the whisky mixture.

This mixture, taken in moderation (30 ml/day for a month) is said to produce interesting results. Remember this recipe comes from cold Canada where they probably need lots of encouragement to disrobe.

I notice I am being a little sexist here and not discussing specific female aphrodisiacs. My favourite herbal writer, Jeanne Rose, has a whole chapter in her book *Herbs and Things* on aphrodisiacs. My favourite of her suggestions involves honey and this and other suggestions of hers may go part of the way to explain why Jeanne was banned from the American Herb Society!

If you have a sexual problem, do not be afraid to discuss this with your medical adviser.

Appetite

Generations of people have used herbs to stimulate or reduce appetite. The bitter tasting herbs such as quassia, chicory, hops, horehound and gentian have always been thought to stimulate appetite. When I was growing up, the local doctor always used to prescribe stout to build one up after an operation or illness. I remember the bitter taste of the stout that my mother gave me after an appendix operation. Interestingly, recent research has shown that bitter tastes do stimulate the appetite. Simon Mills says that bitter tastes:

> lead to the release from the gut wall into the bloodstream, of a hormone called gastrin. This hormone has a number of effects including increasing the flow of gastric juices, bile, insulin, and glucagon all of which are beneficial to digestion.[7]

So, here is the excuse for drinking bitter beer (remember horehound beer?), tonic bitters and stout. But don't do as I did when I was twelve, and add lemonade to the stout. As Mills says, it is the bitter taste that is doing us the good!

Many of us feel that we have the opposite problem and have too good an appetite. To reduce appetite you must chew 'Meetin' Seed' or grandmother's fennel.

Grandmother's Fennel

When I was a tiny bit of a girl
In the country meeting-house,
Where I was expected to sit as still
As a frightened little mouse,
Perhaps I did not relish the feast
Which the good old parson spread
But I did enjoy my grandmother's treat
Of a fragrant Fennel head.

I'm a grandmother now, myself, you know,
But the dainty blue-eyed girl,
Who sits by my side in a city church
With her feathers all in a curl,
Will never know in her Greenaway gown
Exactly the joy I knew,
As I tasted the fresh sweet 'Meetin' Seed'
That in grandmother's garden grew.

Anon.

In days gone by when one fasted before going to church and then sat through long, long sermons (is there any other kind?), one took along some 'Meetin' Seed'. This was a little collection of seed, such as fennel and caraway, that one chewed secretively in church to stop the tummy growling. I have often found myself picking fennel seed from the garden when lunch is overdue. I like them when they are still a little green and juicy before they dry out on the bush. They have a flavour like sweet liquorice. Children love them. Mine call fennel's umbrella-like heads 'eating flowers' and never miss a chance to nibble on them.

'Hast thou ought in thy purse?' quod he.
'Any hot spices?'
'I have pepper, pionies,' quod she, 'and a pound of garlike
A ferdyng worth of fennel seed for fasting days'

Piers Plowman

Arthritis and Rheumatism

Arthritis and rheumatism are terrible words as each is so vague and describes a multitude of diseases. Rheumatism can mean a twinge or inflammation in a joint. Arthritis can also be a twinge in the joint but can include crippling, disfiguring and even deadly disorders. There are dozens of herbs used to alleviate these complaints, however a complete look at them is beyond the scope of this book. There are a number of alternative and popular main stream medical books on the subject which are well worth a read if you have been diagnosed with one of these complaints.

My own theory is that there has to be a food allergy or intolerance factor involved in arthritis and rheumatism. There is, however, no universal 'good' diet for arthritis. What is good for one person may be disastrous for another.

One day, I was in the nursery talking to a very fit looking man, about 50 years of age, I thought. He told me that for the previous 10 years he had been crippled by arthritis. He went to a Chinese herbalist who advised him to give up all fruit! He did and the effect was amazing! No more arthritis! I was amazed, too, to find out this 'fit 50 year old' was in fact over 70 years of age! He was obviously doing something right (for him). I wondered if giving up all fruit was necessary. Perhaps only one or two fruits or a fruit family (like citrus) could have caused the problem.

Plants in the potato or Solanaceae family (tomatoes, capsicums and chilli peppers) and those containing salicylates (oranges and strawberries) can produce arthritis-like symptoms in some people, especially if eaten to excess. A friend, a 40-year-old nurse and mother of two, was getting very depressed as she could hardly walk due to the painful swellings in her joints. She saw a life ahead as an invalid. I asked her what she was eating.

'Oh, not much. I'm on a diet.'

'What does the diet consist of?'

'Just tomatoes.'

'How many tomatoes?' I asked.

'Two or three kilos a day.'

I suggested she refrain from the Solanaceae family of plants, which includes the tomato and potato. After six weeks on a no-tomato, no-potato diet she had completely recovered.

The academic research on diet and arthritis, to paraphrase, goes a little like this: 'We tested 100 people on a [insert your favourite diet here]. There was no change in 95% of patients. Diets therefore do not help arthritis.'

This is the conclusion demanded by the statistics and the scientific method. The interesting result of the research is that five people totally recovered! These five swear by the diet, stay on it and tell all their friends, not realising that what helps them may not help all their friends (or may only help one in twenty).

Usually there is a great deal of resistance to changing one's diet. Often one's favourite foods are the foods at fault. Unfortunately, you will have to sort out your own poisons. Look first at foods you crave or foods that you eat every day of the year or in large quantities. The Chinese say we should only eat foods in season, thus giving our bodies nine months or more to excrete any accumulated toxins from one plant. When we eat the same thing every day, they say, plant toxins can build up. This varies greatly from person to person, perhaps because we all have different metabolisms. What is food to one person can be a toxin to another!

Herbs that can help or hinder the management of the symptoms of arthritis and rheumatism are discussed below.

Anti-inflammatory Herbs

Feverfew, Meadowsweet and Camomile

Teas of camomile and meadowsweet are especially useful for inflamed stomachs caused by food intolerance. All are soothing and anti-inflammatory. Meadowsweet may also help with pain and inflammation in joints.

Camomile, Rosemary and Wintergreen Essential Oils

These can make excellent rubs for inflamed joints. Make your own rub by adding 10% of essential oils (such as rosemary, lavender, camomile or wintergreen) to olive oil. Use this as an 'ointment' when necessary. All these essential oils have either anti-inflammatory (reduce inflammation) or hyperaemic (cause better local blood circulation) effects. Most wintergreen oils available today are synthetic and are not plant derived. Commercial sports and rheumatism rubs are generally based on synthetic wintergreen or synthetic camphor.

Aloe arborescens

We had an old timer come to the nursery one day bringing along his miracle plant for arthritis. For years he had been crippled with joint pain until he was told to rub the sap of this plant into his painful joints. The pain disappeared. Since then he has been telling everyone he could about his cure. The plant was *Aloe arborescens*, a commonly grown ornamental aloe. Since that time we have had many people get quick relief from arthritis pain by rubbing the juice of the plant into painful and inflamed joints.

Blood Purifying Herbs

Blood purifying herbs are herbs that help the body eliminate its toxins.

Violet Leaves

The leaves of the common mauve violet, *Viola odorata*, sometimes called Prince or Princess of Wales, can be added to salads. They have an interesting lettuce-like flavour. *(See Cancer section.)*

Dandelion

This, too, can be added to salads. Other blood purifying herbs include nettle and burdock. Most of these can be taken as teas or alcoholic tinctures which can be purchased from your health food store or naturopath.

Celery Seed and Juniper Berry

These are blood purifying because they are kidney stimulants and have a diuretic effect. You should avoid prolonged use of them if you have any kidney problems. The good news is that juniper berry is used to make gin. (A good excuse for a medicinal gin and tonic daily!) If you would prefer to avoid alcohol, juniper berry essential oil can be used. Put a few drops in a bath, rub some into an inflamed joint, or the inflamed area can be soaked in warm water with six to ten drops of juniper berry oil added. Gin was one of the first herbal medicines for rheumatism and gout. Gin made from juniper berries is a powerful kidney stimulant. Juniper helps the body remove uric acid and so is helpful for many forms of arthritis.

Celery seed is a diuretic and, like all diuretics, should be used in moderation and with caution. You might also like to make yourself some celery soup or just eat fresh celery, although celery seeds do contain medicinal properties that the stems don't. One year, enthused with the religion of self-sufficiency, Jan and I collected our own celery seed. The seed had to be rubbed off the plant with our fingers. To our amazement, very soon our fingers were totally numb. The seed had acted as a local anaesthetic! The numbness lasted for some hours.

Celery
This is excellent for rheumatism. Eat it any way you can, and as often as you like. One way of preparing it is to cut celery into pieces and boil in water until soft, then drink the water. Put fresh milk, with a little flour and nutmeg, into a saucepan with boiled celery, and serve warm with pieces of toast.

Anti-oxidant Herbs

Anti-oxidants slow down the wear and tear on the body and so assist in the treatment of rheumatism and arthritis. Herbs that have some reputation here include comfrey, garlic, ginseng and possibly fo ti tung. Non-herbal anti-oxidants include vitamin C (non-acidic is best) and vitamin E, and trace elements such as germanium (found in Aloe vera and comfrey) and selenium, for which a prescription is needed in Australia.

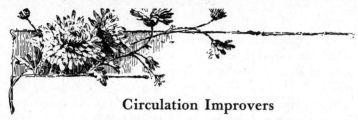

Circulation Improvers

Warming herbs that promote blood supply to the afflicted joint include cayenne pepper (a no-no if you suspect a Solanaceae allergy), ginseng, wintergreen and rosemary. Essential oils of rosemary and wintergreen make excellent rubs for inflamed joints. Use them rubbed into the joint neat or use one part essential oil to ten parts olive (preferably) or other carrier oil such as sweet almond oil.

Immune System Stimulants

Immune system stimulants are herbs which have remarkable power to boost the immune system. The immune system is the system of defence our bodies use to fight infection. Every day we come into contact with all sorts of disease-causing bacteria and viruses. Every day, unknown to us, the immune system fights and kills these invaders. We get sick when something slips through our defences.

Echinacea
Echinacea, also known as coneflower or Blackeyed Susan, is the most commonly used herb to help stimulate the immune system. It has a pretty, daisy-like flower. The roots can be collected and made into a tea or preserved in alcohol (vodka or gin) and a little is drunk daily. The tea is the safe form for small children. Don't go overboard with Echinacea; more is not necessarily better. Some herbalists recommend taking it for a few months then stopping for a few months.

Pokeroot
Pokeroot or inkweed is another herb or common weed which can be used for arthritis, but it can be irritating and is best taken under the supervision of a medical herbalist. Traditionally, pokeroot *(Phytolacca)* berries were soaked in wine or brandy by early American settlers and taken daily for rheumatism. Apparently it is quite a brew! Be careful with this one, as pokeroot can be toxic and the old timers are a bit vague on quantities.

A tincture of the ripe berries in brandy or wine is a great remedy in cases of sciatic, or chronic rheumatisms, and should be used freely in all such cases.[8]

Golden Seal *(Hydrastis canadensis)*

Golden Seal contains berberine, a chemical that has been shown in a number of modern studies[9] to stimulate the immune system's ability to fight infection. Golden Seal is not a common herb. It grows best in cold climates and is very expensive to buy. As it has some unusual side effects (see pregnancy section) it is best taken under the supervision of a trained herbalist.

Liquorice

Liquorice comes a close second to ginseng as the most used herb of the Chinese. Until recently, in the West it has been regarded merely as a flavour. Pizzorno and Murray[10] state that liquorice has been shown in animal studies not only to stimulate the bacteria-killing activity of the immune system (macrophage activity), but also to assist the body to produce interferon. Interferon is a chemical produced by the body that helps fight viral and bacterial infections.

Tummy Herbs

If you suspect digestive problems associated with arthritis you might like to include some tummy herbs in your diet. Camomile tea and peppermint tea, Golden Seal, comfrey, slippery elm bark powder, liquorice, meadowsweet, Aloe vera gel (preferably fresh) and feverfew. All these have a soothing, anti-inflammatory or tonic effect on the stomach.

Calming Herbs

Reducing stress levels is very important for any immune system disorder. Stress of any kind can weaken our immune system. Avoid it where possible, or take steps to deal with it. Calming herbs are not the cure for stress, but they can be helpful and healing. Camomile, hops, valerian, and skullcap are calming, sedative herbs. Try including a tea of one or all of these in your daily routine. Some tea manufacturers make special calming tea which is a blend of several calming herbs. Treat yourself to a massage with some essential oil of lavender, one of the most relaxing of all the fragrances. Massaging, in itself, is very good for stress. Psychologically, the touch or stroking from another can be a powerful calmer and healer. Try using traditional calming fragrances such as lavender or rose geranium in a warm bath or spa and relax for half an hour with a good book. After exams my wife used to repair to such a scented bath, armed with a book of poetry, a detective novel, a plate of oysters and a bottle of red. She claimed it was wondrously calming.

Plants to Avoid

Some plant families seem to aggravate some people and we don't know why. Most conventional doctors don't believe this. Most naturopaths do. Only time will tell who is right. Plants are related to each other. Like human families, they often share a similar (botanic) name, although not always. They can look very similar or surprisingly different. For some arthritis sufferers, problem plant families are the Solanaceae (nightshade plant family), which includes potatoes, peppers and tomatoes, or the Citrus family, which includes oranges, limes, lemons and grapefruit.

Chocolate, strawberries, cow's milk and some food additives may aggravate arthritis in some people. This is something you will have to work out for yourself. Some researchers suggest that persons suffering from systemic lupus erythematosus (SLE) should not eat alfalfa. Sulphur can trigger some rarer forms of arthritis where there is a genetic predisposition (i.e. you inherited it from your parents). Sulphur is used as a preservative in everything from wine to dried fruit. Try an allergy elimination diet, especially if symptoms include some or all of these: low-grade fever, depression, lethargy, chronic diarrhoea, migraine headaches, skin problems, ringing in the ears or malaise. Be warned though, it is probably the food you crave that is the problem!

Management of Arthritis

Finding out what causes your arthritis is a personal odyssey which could take some time and continual assessment of the best direction to take. It is best to find a doctor who is interested in alternative medicine or a herbalist you can work with. The conventional treatment for this disorder sometimes involves prescribing regular cortisone-type drugs which, in time, can only depress the immune system. This seems to me to be a crazy approach. Cortisone might be acceptable in the short term or to help sufferers through a bad attack, but it cannot be a long-term solution. There are many suggestions for you to explore in the preceding paragraphs. Take heart; think positive.

Athlete's Foot (tinea pedis)

Those itchy, scaly, smelly, red bits between your toes are caused by a fungus. It is quite common, especially in tropical areas, with up to 7% of men and 4% of women suffering some form of it. Keep the toes clean and dry, and swab daily with neat tea tree and/or lavender oil. Mild cases should clear in seven to ten days. It is a good idea to keep painting the infected area with tea tree oil for a while after the infection looks as though it has cleared, as the fungus that causes this complaint is very persistent. Once the fungus is around the home it is very hard to eradicate. It is thought that the fungus can be spread from bathroom floors, mats and towels and can therefore spread through a family. Liberally sprinkle the floor with your favourite essential oil. A cottonwool ball with a few drops of tea tree oil should be put in shoes after wearing them. Very severe cases of tinea have been cured with neat essential oil of garlic. This is a remedy for the very desperate.

Mild tinea seems to respond to a daily treatment of comfrey ointment. Seal over the area that is peeling, having first washed and dried your feet very carefully. Continue for a week and mild cases seem to disappear. The nineteenth century chemist William Whitla writes that:

> Thymol, Menthol, and nearly every Essential B.P. Oil will cure [tinea/ringworm] if persisted in and cause very little irritation ... the secret of success consists in the patient continuance of the same remedy.[11]

Bad Breath

Halitosis, or bad breath, can be caused by lots of things. Firstly, get your teeth checked by your dentist. If your tonsils are chronically enlarged and infected, try a tea of sage and lemon thyme (a sprig of fresh sage and three of lemon thyme to a cup of hot water). An effective temporary remedy is to add two drops of peppermint oil to a cup of warm water and gargle for a few minutes. Repeat as often as necessary.

A tea made from a fresh sprig of common thyme, rosemary or the afore-mentioned sage or lemon thyme, can also be helpful. These herbs are strong antiseptics and are freshly fragrant. To make a tea, pour a cup of boiling water over a sprig of leaves. Infuse for a few minutes, strain and drink.

Chewing fresh parsley is supposed to get rid of the worst garlic breath. Chewing fresh mint leaves can also be helpful.

Balding

Physicians of the utmost fame,
Were called at once but when they came
They answered as they took their fees
There is no cure for this disease.

Anon.

Rosemary, southernwood and the Australian Aboriginal herb 'old man weed' have been traditionally associated with saving hair. A balding botanist from Monash University is presently testing the Aboriginal remedy!

My experience with rosemary is that it does not restore hair, but it does seem to slow down the process of balding. Rosemary oil rubbed into the scalp increases blood supply to the scalp. Rosemary oil will, therefore, help where poor circulation is the problem. You can also add a few drops of rosemary oil to your shampoos and conditioners.

Bay rum tincture was grandpa's remedy for baldness. The oil which has a delightful fragrance comes from the leaves of the bay rum tree. (There is a beautiful old tree in the Sydney Botanic Gardens.) Like all essential oils, it is antiseptic, invigorating and cleansing. The tincture can be made from 5% bay rum oil in alcohol. The old recipes usually included other essential oils, or chemicals like cantharidin to irritate or stimulate the scalp.

Barber's Bay Rum [12]

Oil of bay 30 ml	Oil of Lemon 2 drops
Borax 1 pinch	Alcohol 60 ml
Oil of Cinnamon 2 drops	Water to 4.5 L
Oil of Clove 1 drop	Talc 120 g

Rub the oils with the talc in a mortar until they are thoroughly mixed, then add the borax. Then add the alcohol and transfer to a bottle. Rinse out the mortar with some water and add to the alcohol-oil mixture. Shake thoroughly and add the rest of the water to make 1 gallon [4.5 L]. Allow to stand twenty-four hours with frequent shaking, and filter.

The old books suggest southernwood ashes. Southernwood is a pretty aromatic herb, looking a little like a miniature Christmas tree. The herb is burned and the ashes rubbed into the scalp. As it is too much trouble for all but the most desperate, we have no first-hand information on this very old remedy's efficacy. Interestingly, at least three old Irish remedies for baldness involve using ashes—of a mouse, a raven and a 'sally' tree. I wonder what the common ingredient in all these ashes might be?

A traditional Chinese remedy involves mashing fresh ginger, warming it and spreading it on the bald patch. We have seen sillier Chinese remedies work and how many bald Chinese have you seen? Essential oil of ginger might be easier to use and worth trying too. This remedy probably works in the same way as rosemary oil—promoting blood supply to the scalp. (*See dandruff.*)

Although not yet conclusive, recent Japanese research about baldness points the accusing finger at high animal fat diets. More and more Japanese are becoming bald as the traditional Japanese diet is changing to include more animal fats. This is is perhaps the best reason of all to go on a low cholesterol diet, Dad. This may also explain why baldness is more common in the West than in Asia.

> Orientals traditionally consume comparatively small amounts of animal fats even at present. This results in a moderate sebaceous gland size... As a result, hairs grow thick and healthy, and little tendency to male pattern baldness is observed.[13]

Blackheads

This is a recipe from an old medical herbal.

> Before going to bed, rub lemon juice over blackheads. Wait until morning to wash off the juice with cool water. Repeat several evenings in a row and you'll see a big improvement in the skin.[14]

Bleeding

Blood means an emergency. The reason people faint at the sight of blood is that you're not supposed to see it. It should stay inside the body. If it's outside and splashing around, this is a tip off that something is wrong. Urgent action is required.

James Gormon, *First Aid for Hypochondriacs*

Astringent Herbs

Astringent herbs stop or reduce bleeding because of their tannin content, which acts to 'curdle' protein molecules (just like boiling an egg). The very large number of astringent herbs includes: agrimony, Lady's Mantle, blackberry leaves, plantain, comfrey, cayenne, geranium (cranesbill), lemon juice, raspberry leaf and any part of a deciduous tree.

Self Heal

The appropriately named self heal *(Prunella vulgaris)* is a pretty little ground cover that must have saved many a medieval swain who had an accident with his scythe while harvesting the crops. In the days before ambulances and blood transfusions, herbs such as self heal had a major place in emergencies. Because astringent herbs saved so many lives by stopping the bleeding, they are all associated with magic and folklore. Today they are relegated to garden ornamentals and we phone for an ambulance for major catastrophes, but for minor 'blooding' (as my infant daughter used to say) try one of the astringent herbs.

Yarrow

Yarrow *(Achillea millefolium)* in folklore was said to be so effective that it even would staunch Achilles' heel! Yarrow is a very effective astringent that stops bleeding. It's ironic that Achilles, who most needed yarrow, should have bequeathed his name to this anti-haemorrhage herb.

   In an emergency, grab a handful of clean leaves of astringent herbs such as yarrow or self heal, bruise them, apply directly to the wound with pressure and ring the ambulance.

Blood Pressure

High

High blood pressure is the sort of condition that needs supervision by your naturopath or doctor. Hypertension (i.e. high blood pressure) is mostly caused by our diet and lifestyle. People living in remote areas of China, New Guinea, the Soloman Islands, etc, show virtually no evidence of essential hypertension. However, when these people migrate to less remote areas and adopt a more 'civilised' diet, the incidence of hypertension increases dramatically.

Some of the herbs that have been shown to help high blood pressure include garlic, mistletoe, olive leaves, valerian, hawthorn (especially good where there is heart weakness and angina), periwinkle *(Vinca minor)*, comfrey, mullein *(Verbascum)* and ginseng. Ginseng must only be taken in small doses at first, over a long period (three to twelve months) as large doses can elevate blood pressure. Discuss the use of these herbs with your herbalist. If you must self-treat, start with garlic or small doses (250 mg a day) of ginseng.

Onions 'thin the blood' and lower blood pressure. They contain adenosine, a chemical that stops blood clotting. People with high levels of fibrinogen—the stuff that starts clots—are more likely to suffer from clots and heart disease. Onions work to dissolve the clots as they form.[15]

Other foods that help lower blood pressure include: mackerel, olive oil, seaweed, yoghurt and Chinese green tea.

Low

> Rosemary Tea will cure a nervous headache and has a beneficial effect on the brain. Its constant use will greatly improve a bad memory. It was recommended by Pliny for failing eyesight. Its stimulating effect on the circulation of the blood makes it useful for the memory and the eyes.[16]

Rosemary tea helps elevate blood pressure. Place a sprig in a cup of hot water, or three to six drops of the essential oil in the bath.

One of our staff took to fresh rosemary tea and started to drink several cups a day. She then started to feel quite 'off'. It turned out that her blood pressure was already a little high and the rosemary tea was making it higher! As my grandfather said 'Moderation in all things, my son'. Actually *he* was never very moderate about much, as I remember.

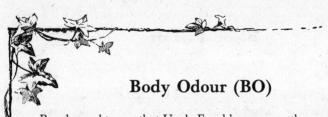

Body Odour (BO)

People used to say that Uncle Frank's nose was the reason he never married 'a good Christian woman'. No girl ever smelt right to him.[17]

As most essential oils are excellent bactericides, small amounts (one or two drops) can be used under arms and other areas to reduce body odour. A few drops of lavender essential oil under the arms will stop odour for about six hours in warm climates. If you mix the oil with a little vaseline or sorbolene, it will last even longer. This is very useful to people with allergies to antiperspirants or deodorants. We have a number of customers who use essential oils in this way, including a young baker who works near hot ovens all day. It is interesting that these people are allergic to very small amounts of chemical in the antiperspirants, and yet can use these quite strong concentrations of herbs with impunity. Some lemon oils (lemongrass) are now being made into natural deodorants. Lemon oils are sometimes difficult to use neat on the skin. Lavender essential oil is a much nicer, safer and easier herb to use.

Boils

The biblical remedy for boils was a poultice of fresh figs:

> And Isaiah said, 'Take a lump of figs'.
> And they took and laid it on the boil, and he recovered.

2 Kings 20:7.

Boils are local inflammation of the hair roots caused by bacterial (staphylococcal) infection. A cluster of boils is referred to as a carbuncle. If boils are numerous and severe and do not respond quickly to natural treatment, seek medical treatment as the infection can spread quickly and can be very debilitating.

Many herbalists feel that boils are a symptom of the body's inability to deal with toxins, the result of a sluggish liver, inefficient kidneys, poor nutrition, constipation or blood sugar problems. Do discuss your general health with your medical adviser if boils are frequent.

To treat boils, comfrey tea and other blood purifying herbs should be taken, and comfrey ointment with an antiseptic liberally applied to the infected area if the boil has not come to a head. Many of the better comfrey ointments contain antiseptic essential oils or Golden Seal. If the boil erupts, keep the area clean with soap and warm water, wash with a strong solution (twenty or more drops to a cup of water) of lavender essential oil (not perfume oil). Apply the comfrey only to the edges of the infection at this stage; otherwise, the comfrey will seal the wound and now allow the infection to drain. Bandage loosely when the area is totally drained and cleansed (two to three days) and keep applying comfrey for some weeks to prevent scarring and to speed healing.

Broken Bones

Obviously, broken bones need medical attention and to speed healing, the herb comfrey is unsurpassed. We once had an Afghan hound called Bekki (actually Rebecca Bianca Myffymy Bailes). Like most Afghan pups she seemed to have a self-destruct button. Her worst accident occurred when she ran into the back wheel of a speeding car! Her back leg was broken in several spots. The vet recommended we destroy her as she would never walk again. We had the vet put the leg in a half cast. (We knew from previous experience that full casts just don't work on Afghans; the leg swells.)

We then slathered the leg in masses of comfrey ointment every night. We gave Bekki as much comfrey to eat as possible. She hated taking tablets, but I battled with her to take them. After one especially frustrating time forcing tablets down her throat, I decided to give up. I held out my hand full of comfrey root tablets and to my amazement she started eating them from my hand. Her leg completely recovered after about 12 weeks. When we took her back to the vet, he was dumbfounded. 'It was this leg that was broken, wasn't it?' he said, pointing to the wrong leg! We told him what we had done. Sadly, he just dismissed our treatment with 'Well, some dogs have amazing powers of recovery'.

A little while after Bekki's leg was completely cured she began to refuse to take any more comfrey tablets. I started to battle with her again. Forcing Afghans to do anything they don't want to do is always a battle royal. I thought as the leg had been so bad I should continue with the comfrey. It then dawned on my slow brain that she took them from me when she needed them; she now had decided she didn't need them any more. The battle stopped.

Comfrey has a reputation as a bone healer dating back to medieval times. Its very old names include Knitbone, Consound and Nipbone. During the crusades, it was planted at every watering hole along the traveller's road. If a good knight fell off his horse and broke anything, he had comfrey at hand. In fact, comfrey root was spread on a bandage wrapped around the set broken limb. This apparently hardened like a plaster cast. It is said that it was the best cast ever invented as it gave a little with swelling and the chemicals in the comfrey promoted rapid healing.

> In the days when popular opinion refused to consider herbal medicines the idea that Comfrey could knit a broken bone was much scoffed at, yet within recent years, leading surgeons have discovered that the powdered root, if dissolved in water to form a thick mucilage, is of great value in bleedings and fractures. There is a story which seems well authenticated that one of the men who had charge of Twickenham Lock broke the bone of his little finger, and by some carelessness it was improperly set. For two months he felt the fractured bones grinding against each other, and the pain was so great he became almost demented.
>
> One day, so he said, he saw a doctor who was a local celebrity, and told him of his agony. The doctor pointed to a herb on the river bank. 'You see that Comfrey,' he said. 'Take a piece of the root, champ it, put it about your finger and wrap it up.' The old man did so and was completely cured.[18]

Bruises

Arnica is the classic herb for bruises. Its effects are miraculous. A jar of arnica ointment is essential in the herbal medicine chest. I once managed to jam my foot under a large log I was cutting with a chainsaw. The inevitable result was that by bedtime I could hardly walk on my swollen, black and blue foot. Jan then suggested I try my own remedies and use arnica. I thought it was probably too late as arnica ointment should be applied quickly to a bruise. However, after two days the bruise faded and quickly disappeared! If the skin is broken use comfrey ointment. I have never worked out why traditional herbalists recommend not using arnica on broken skin, but the advice comes up repeatedly and we do follow it.

 Culpeper recommends boiling a good handful of violet *(Viola odorata)* leaves and applying this 'strong tea' (called a 'decoction') to bruises.[19]

Burns

Minor burns and scalds

A local chef thanked us for an Aloe vera plant which we had given him a year previously. He found he was often splashing himself with hot oil and on at least two occasions aloe had kept his restaurant open after he'd burned himself badly.

Aloe vera is incredible on burns. For some burns, it immediately takes away the pain! Plunging the burn into cold water is the best treatment because it stops the burns becoming deeper. Because of its allantoin and germanium content, Aloe vera immediately promotes healing and is also antiseptic and astringent. There is no better first aid for burns.

Two varieties of Aloe vera are commonly sold in nurseries: the small Indian aloe with orange flowers and the larger true Aloe vera of commerce with its yellow flowers. Both work well but the true aloe is preferred. I am told that some varieties of aloe (there are hundreds) contain soothing natural cortisone-like substances which seem to help skin problems, but perhaps should not be used on burns. Always make sure, therefore, that you are using the appropriate plant. Remember the true Aloe vera has yellow flowers. The Indian aloe, which is also good to use on burns, has orange flowers and is usually the one sold at nurseries and school fetes as 'true aloe'. Just because an aloe seems to help skin complaints, it is not necessarily an Aloe vera.

Grow your aloe indoors in a sunny, warm spot if you live in a frosty area. It will happily grow outside in warm climates.

Using fresh Aloe vera is simplicity itself. Break open a large old leaf and apply lots of the inner gel directly to the burn as often as necessary—at least three applications in the first hour—to take away the pain.

Neat lavender essential oil has also been used on burns with great success. This was first discovered when a perfumer, who burnt herself in the laboratory, plunged her hand into a container of pure essential oil of lavender. The consequent healing was apparently miraculous. Recently, similar experiments with Australian tea tree oil have shown promising results.

Serious burns, especially those to young children or to a large area of the body should receive immediate medical attention.

Major Burns and Scalds

The most severe burns are called third degree. In third degree burns, all layers of skin are destroyed and the skin can look white or charred. Strangely, the pain of third degree burns may not be as severe as more minor burns. This is because the pain does not register in the brain, since the pain receptors in the skin have been destroyed. The first thing to do here is call an ambulance and follow current first aid procedures. It is important to get medical attention as soon as possible. Do not use herbal ointments or preparations on the burn.

Many people swear by Bach Flower Rescue Remedy which is supposed to help shock. A few drops can be given if the patient is conscious and not vomiting. I have seen many people get amazing results with this remedy, but I am personally at a loss to see why it should work at all.

Burping (belching)

Try a cup of peppermint and/or camomile tea after your meal, or soak a tablet (preferably dolomite, but garlic or a vitamin tablet can be used) with two to three drops of peppermint oil and take after your meal. Eating slowly also helps. Avoid drinking a lot of fluid with meals.

Calming Herbs

(See also Sleep Herbs)

A few drops of lavender, rose geranium or camomile essential oil in the bath are helpful.

Rose geranium

Just after starting The Fragrant Garden, Jan and I took a car load of scented geraniums (mostly rose) to the Hawkesbury Agricultural College for a spring display. It was a cool but sunny day and we had the windows of the car fully wound up. The car filled with wonderful rose fragrance from the plants. However, every ten minutes we had to stop, walk around the car and swap drivers. We were both so tired, it took hours to get to Hawkesbury. When we returned home I looked up the uses of rose geranium. All the old herbals suggested its use in sleep pillows! Rose geranium, as we had discovered, was a very effective sleep herb!

To use this old remedy, rose geranium leaves can be dried and made into a pot-pourri for the bedroom. Add about 10% orris root powder or oak moss to help hold and 'fix' the fragrance and splash in a few millilitres of essential oil of rose geranium. This pot-pourri will surprise you, as not only will it help you sleep, but the fragrance will improve as the pot-pourri gets older!

Hops

The fragrance of hops is also calming. Hops are the flowers of the hop plant which is used to make beer. (Interestingly, hops are in the same botanical family as cannabis—Cannabinaceae). Hops are inexpensive and you can buy them from health food or brewing supply shops. Add a handful of these to your rose geranium pot-pourri every few weeks. (Hops lose their effectiveness after a while.) This will make a great sleep pot-pourri. Put it all in a large bowl so that you can add to it from time to time. Add some dried rose petals from your garden too. Be sure to keep your orris root or oak moss to at least 10% of the total weight. Sleep pillows used to be made by stuffing a large pillow with hops and sleeping on this.

In the early days of The Fragrant Garden, we had a little mud-brick shop. One warm summer day I found myself nodding off behind the counter (customers were harder to find then). My wife came in and 'gently' prodded me into the garden. After a while, and a cup of coffee, I came back into the shop to find Jan nodding off. We commiserated with each other that we needed a holiday and were both obviously seriously exhausted!

A little while later Jan came out of the shop holding at arm's length a huge plastic bag of hops. She had found these tucked behind the counter and this was what was putting us to sleep! Since then I have read that it is the yellow dust on the hop flowers that makes you drowsy. Yet these hops were in a sealed plastic bag and only a little fragrance could escape.

> It is impossible to speak too highly of hops as inducers of sleep. Their narcotic properties are very strong, and instances have been known in which quite wideawake people, going into an oast house where hops are being dried, have been impelled to sit down anywhere and go into a long and sound sleep.[20]

Remember, if you have a sleep pillow or a sleep pot-pourri, add new hops every few weeks because as they start to lose their smell they also seem to lose their effectiveness.

> The hop pillow should be a muslin bag, smaller than the usual pillow case, which must be loosely filled with dried hops. This hop pillow is of the greatest value with nervous patients, and all who are highly strung or unable to sleep from any cause. The hops should be renewed every month.[21]

If you make hop pillows too small they may not be very effective. If you make them too large you may not be able to stand the smell. This is why sweet-smelling herbs such as rose and lavender are added.

Valerian

Valerian is probably the strongest legal herbal tranquilliser. I was with a group of inquisitive males inspecting a unique dome house some years ago. The owner offered us all a cup of tea but then discovered he only had herb tea—to be precise, valerian tea. We had our tea and after a while one of our party fell asleep. The rest of us, yawning, made our departure. It occurred to me some time later that our host's running out of ordinary (camellia) tea just might have been intentional. It is an excellent way of getting rid of unwanted guests! Valerian loses its effectiveness with age. Keep it in an air-tight jar.

Lemon tree

In India, the leaves of the lemon tree are used as a tea at night to help relax tension and aid sleep. Several leaves are gently simmered in one and a half cups of water for 15 to 20 minutes. Sweeten with a little honey if you wish. This is a delightful, tasty and inexpensive tea (if you grow your own lemon tree). A few lemon leaves can be added to, and will improve the flavour of, valerian tea.

Cancer

(See also Immune System)

Cancer epidemiologists have claimed that up to 90% of all human cancers are induced by, or associated with, environmental factors including diet.[22]

Yellow vegetables, such as carrots, help protect our bodies from cancer. It has been estimated that if everyone in the United States ate one carrot a day there would be 15 000 to 20 000 fewer lung cancer deaths a year in that country![23] Carrots are better cooked for a minute or two in a

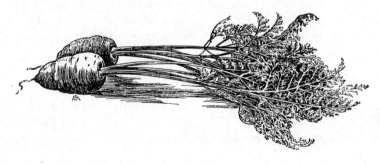

little boiling water. A little cooking releases more carotene. Too much cooking softens the carrots and destroys the carotene.

Germanium is a trace element, actually a metal, which is found concentrated in the stems of a number of plants. It has been shown in modern clinical tests to normalise and regulate immune system function.[24a]

> Germanium is a potent anti-cancer agent in humans with no major known side effects up to the concentrations of several grams a day employed in clinical studies.[24b]

If you would like to include more germanium in your diet, the following plants contain the highest amounts:

Shelf fungus *(Trametes cinnabarina)*	800–2000 parts per million (ppm)
Garlic	754 ppm
Ginseng	250–320 ppm
Susi *(Angelica pubescens)*	262 ppm
Sanzukon *(Codonopsis tangshen)*	257 ppm
Waternut *(Trapa japonica)*	239 ppm
Comfrey	152 ppm
Boxthorn seed *(Lycium chinense)*	124 ppm
Wisteria gall *(Wisteria floribunda)*	108 ppm
Aloe	77 ppm
Pearl barley *(Hordeum vulgare)*	50 ppm

Aloe vera

Aloe is a folk remedy for many types of cancer including skin cancer, liver, nose and stomach cancer. Externally it can be used in the same way as for burns. To use internally, peel the Aloe leaves and remove the yellow sap because it tastes terrible. Leave the sap only if you can stand it, as it is medicinal, if a little laxative. Blend the gel from a large leaf with a cup or two of apple or other juice in the blender. It must be very well mixed in the blender! Hold your nose and drink it down. You might prefer to peel the Aloe, place a large chunk into a litre of water and allow it to sit in the refrigerator for around six to eight hours before you drink the water.

Comfrey

There are several anecdotal instances where comfrey has been involved in a cancer cure. Some of these are reported in medical journals.[a] Several of my customers have used comfrey ointment to cure skin cancers or suspected cancers. The ointment is usually applied daily for four to eight weeks. One customer, however, used a fresh leaf taped on to the suspected cancer on his hand with a band-aid. His suspected cancer disappeared within four weeks. The herb, comfrey, is a complex chemical factory. The roots contain mucilage, allantoin, symphytine, echimidine, isobauerenol, beta-sitosterol, lasiocarpine, tannins and a range of other chemicals including pyrrolizidine alkaloids (although these are mainly contained in the leaves). Alkaloids are a group of chemicals that give us a number of powerful modern medicines. Taken (internally) to excess, however, they are very toxic. Incidentally, alkaloids are mostly found in tropical rainforest plants, but comfrey grows happily in much colder climates so long as it has plenty of water.

Soya bean

The latest plant to be included in the cancer-protective category is the humble soya bean. *New Scientist* reports that women may substantially reduce the risk of breast cancer by consuming soya bean products like soya milk or tofu (the fermented soya bean curd).[25]

Violets

> Violets secrete a soft substance called mucilage which is useful in cases of . . . inflammation and irritation of the stomach and intestine. In the official medical records there is a case of a man who cured himself of cancer of the throat by infusions and compresses of Violets.[26]

Violets are one of the best blood purifying herbs. Maude Grieve and Maurice Mességué, two of the greatest herbalists of this century, speak glowingly of the humble violet, although they are cautious in recommending its use for cancer.

Of late years, preparations of fresh Violet leaves have been used both internally and externally in the treatment of cancer, and though the British Pharmacopoeia does not uphold the treatment, it specifies how they are employed. From other sources it is stated that Violet leaves have been used with benefit to allay the pain in cancerous growths, especially in the throat, which no other treatment relieved, and several reputed cures have been recorded.[27]

Maude Grieve, in her 1931 classic, *A Modern Herbal*, gives specific instructions for making violet tea (70 g fresh leaves to 600 ml boiling water).[28] Interestingly, violets have a very long tradition of being used for cancer. Culpeper says: 'the green leaves are used with other herbs to make plasters and poultices for inflammation and swellings and to ease all pain.'[29]

Catherine Booth (the wife of the founder of the Salvation Army) is said to have used violet leaves to ease the pain of her advanced cancer. Nelson Coon mentions the case of Lady Margaret Marsham, whose throat was closed by a malignant growth. External infusions of violet leaves were made and the cancer apparently disappeared very quickly.[30]

> The Violet plant, as far back as 500 B.C., was used in poultice form as a cure for surface cancer. It was used in 18th century England for the same purpose. And now only months ago—a letter from a farmer in Michigan tells me how he used the Violet plant as a skin cancer remedy. When the remedy was tried on a cancerous mouse here at the Institute, we found that it did damage the cancer.[31]

There are many varieties of violet on the market at the moment. Commonly 'General Herricks', the large florist's violet, is sold incorrectly in some nurseries as *Viola odorata*. This is not the one usually recommended for helping treat cancer. The small old-fashioned, mauve garden violet of grandma's garden (Prince of Wales) with small, pretty, fragrant, violet-blue flowers is the one that has been used for centuries for healing. Other violets may work as well, but no-one has really done the necessary research on violet leaves for which the repeated claims over the centuries cry out.

Violets are simplicity themselves to take. Pick several leaves and infuse them in boiling water and drink. I often have violet leaf tea when I have the flu. Its 'nothing' flavour is strangely invigorating and 'moreish'. Perhaps my body is craving what it knows is good for it. Fresh violet leaves can also be picked from the garden, torn and added to a salad. They are quite tasty with a dressing.

Colon Cancer

Recent research has shown that calcium supplements in the region of 1250 mg a day reduce the risk of colon cancer.

> We think Calcium binds bile and fatty acids, reducing their irritation to the colon lining and thus decreasing the proliferation of cells. The result is a lower risk of colon cancer.[32]

We all should be having 1000 mg or more of calcium a day. (Post-menopausal women should have 1500 mg a day). If you don't eat milk products it is difficult to get this much, unless you eat sardines or the bones of salmon. Many soya milks are enriched with calcium and are also a good source.

The risk of colon cancer can also be reduced, for some, with a diet low in fats and high in fibre.

Lung Cancer

> Cigarette smoking is the major known cause of lung cancer, and smoking cessation would be of more benefit than change in any other single behaviour.

> Archives of International Medicine, 1980[33]

> Tobacco, divine, rare, superexcellent tobacco, which goes beyond all their panaceas, potable gold, and philosophers stones, a sovereign remedy to all diseases... But, as it is commonly abused by most men, which take it as tinkers do ale, 'tis a plague, a mischief, a violent purger of goods, lands, health, hellish, devilish, and damned tobacco, the ruin and overthrow of body and soul.

> Robert Burton, 1577[34]

People who eat lots of green and yellow vegetables can reduce their lung cancer risk by as much as 50%. These vegetables contain masses of vitamin A and C.

Figs

Cancer seems to be less prevalent in areas where figs are eaten. New research is just breaking that may show figs to be excellent in the fight against cancer. Japanese scientists at the Institute of Physical and Chemical Research at the Mitsubishi-Kasei Institute of Life Sciences in Tokyo have isolated an anticancer chemical from figs and used it to treat cancer patients.[35]

The Hebrews have known this for about 3000 years. Look at King Hezekiah! Some modern writers feel that his 'boil' was in fact a cancerous growth.

Other Herbs and Foods

Other herbs and foods that may help protect us from various forms of cancer include apples, apricots, bananas, baked beans, blackberries, buttermilk, cereals (high fibre), dandelion greens, endive, figs, milk (skim), molasses, mustard greens, salmon, sardines and fish (generally), spinach, sweet potatoes, sweet almond oil, shiitake mushrooms, watermelon, yoghurt and cabbage. Probably most of the cabbage family (Brassicaceae) is cancer inhibiting. The family includes broccoli, kale, brussels sprouts, cauliflower, Chinese cabbage, horseradish, watercress, turnip, swede, mustard, kohlrabi and collards. All these foods would be useful to include in the diet. The Chinese don't take herbs when they are sick; they take herbs to stop themselves becoming sick. They are a part of the daily Chinese lifestyle and diet. To me this seems the best way to approach herbal medicine. I believe that if we include a great range of herbs and foods in our diet our bodies will take what they need to keep well and discard the rest.

Honeysuckle leaves, both flowers and stems, have been used in Chinese medicine since the beginnings of recorded history. Ten years ago, one of the main ingredients in honeysuckle, chlorogenic acid, was found to protect experimental animals from carcinogenic chemicals such as nitrosamines and nitrates.[36] So if you are fond of preserved meats and bacon, which contain nitrates, you might like to wash it all down with a cup of honeysuckle tea!

Ultimately, we are responsible for the health of our bodies. If we feed it junk, stress it, call it names (e.g. 'You're no good'), pollute it with environmental toxins, we pay the price. Some of us are lucky and have inherited genes that will cope with a lot of abuse. Others are not so lucky and have to modify their lifestyle accordingly.

Bloodroot *(Sanguinaria canadensis)*
This is a herbaceous perennial in the poppy family growing in the moist deciduous woodlands of North America. The root contains a red sap that oozes when the root is damaged, hence the common name. Bloodroot has a long folk history for the treatment of cancers. The *Lawrence Review of Natural Products* refers to two clinical studies where bloodroot has been investigated for its anti-cancer effects in mice.[37] In another study by Phelan and Juardo, reported in the 1963 *Journal of Surgery*, cancer of the human nose and ear responded to external treatment with a preparation containing bloodroot extract.[38] As the plant contains powerful alkaloids, it should only be used under medical supervision.

It should be noted that the treatment of cancer and all other life-threatening disorders should be supervised by qualified and competent practitioners in whom the patient has confidence.

Candida and Thrush

Candida

Candida albicans is a fungus that causes many people many, many problems. It is a complicated condition beyond the scope of this book. There are a number of good books available just on Candida. It is often prevalent with immune system disorders and it could even be a cause of many food allergies and gut problems ranging from flatulence to malabsorption.

Candida albicans can be killed off temporarily by most essential oils. It is difficult, if not impossible and unnecessary, to eradicate it completely. Try one drop of your favourite oil, such as peppermint, tea tree or lavender mixed with a little slippery elm powder and water or juice. Take this daily until the condition improves. You can gradually increase the amount of essential oil, say to two drops in the second week. I would not recommend any more than 10 drops a day of tea tree oil for an adult without medical supervision.

Most herbal aromatic teas such as peppermint or camomile are helpful, just as ordinary black tea and coffee are not.

Antibiotics tend to kill off the 'good bacteria' (normal bowel flora) as well as the bad, and this allows Candida to multiply unchecked. Lactobacillus acidophilus, found in yoghurt, can replace the good bacteria and therefore alleviate the Candida problems. A drop of tea tree oil on a garlic or dolomite tablet taken three times a day is helpful. Garlic is also a fungicide.

Take steps to strengthen your immune system.

A capful of apple cider vinegar in a cup of water makes for an acid system which Candida doesn't like.

Thrush

Thrush is an infection caused by an overgrowth of fungus (Candida albicans). This condition is often a side effect of long-term cortisone

and/or antibiotic treatments. People with immune system problems are also prone to it. It appears in the mouth, as if the mouth is covered in a layer of curdled milk. There can be a burning pain and bleeding if the layer is removed. Thrush also occurs in the vagina and may cause itching, burning and/or a white discharge.

Use three to eight drops (whatever you can tolerate without irritation) of tea tree or lavender essential oils daily in the bath or as a douche for vaginal thrush. Three to six drops of tea tree or lavender oil to a cup of lukewarm water can be swilled around the mouth several times a day for oral thrush. The oils can cause a mild burning sensation, but this is natural. If you can't stand the flavour, use spearmint or peppermint oils. These are also anti-fungal, although not as strong as tea tree and lavender.

If the condition persists you may have a systemic fungal infection and should discuss treatment of this with a medical professional. Garlic oil or raw garlic cloves, unheated olive oil and tea tree oil are excellent anti-fungals. A sugar-free diet is essential as this yeast-like organism breeds on sugar. Eating natural yoghurt is helpful for many.

Some French doctors suggest douching the vagina with yoghurt. The theory is that the culture in the yoghurt competes with, and may eradicate, the Candida.

> Honey mixed to a paste with borax is the accepted remedy for thrush the white eruption in the mouth . . . the condition only arises at times of great physical exhaustion and in almost every case infants or the aged are the sufferers.

Catarrh

(See also Sinusitis)

> Because of their strong, pungent properties, onions break up mucus congestion. That's why onions also have a reputation as expectorants—agents that prod mucus to move through the lungs and into the throat, where it is coughed up. That too helps the lungs in cases of colds and bronchitis.[39]

Catarrh is mucus running from the sinus cavities in the forehead and below the eyes, down the back of the throat. There are lots of herbal remedies for this complaint. It is probably most often caused by an allergic reaction (to food, pollens, sudden changes in temperature, or pollution) and/or poor diet. Try avoiding anything that comes from a cow (milk, cheese, ice cream, steak) for a few weeks.

Sometimes, sudden changes in temperature will start the nose running or cause a sneezing attack. This can happen when you walk in and out of air-conditioned buildings in summer. Remedies for catarrh include the following:

Place a drop of basil or aniseed oil on the back of your tongue daily for a week.

Place a few drops of The Fragrant Garden Breathe Easy Oil, eucalyptus, thyme or rosemary oil on the pillow at night, or on a light ring or in a scent pot in the room overnight. Scent pots are semi-porous terracotta pots that can be filled with essential or perfume oils; the fragrance slowly evaporates from the outside of the pot, naturally scenting your home or releasing small amounts of medicinal fragrance into the air.

Charms

> Oh, who can tell the hidden
> power of Herbs, and might of
> magic spell.
>
> Edmund Spenser

The old herbalists knew that the most powerful force for healing was the mind. What the mind believes is what happens. One psychiatrist we know says that people talk themselves sick, constantly saying to themselves that they are not well. The process can just as easily be reversed—you can talk yourself well. Take control of that little voice inside you and turn it into a healer.

Early herbalists did not prescribe without an accompanying charm or spell. The words of a spell were spoken or chanted and were an important part of the cure. The herb worked on the body, the charm on the mind. The early Christians had blessings, many of which were adaptations of earlier pagan spells and charms.

Here are some favourite modern charms to add to your repertoire of herbal cures.

A Self Blessing Spell . . .
For Success on an Important Occasion

Steep in a bath
A bowl full of leaves
From three or four
Or five of these:
Marigold, Celery,
Mint and Grass
Nasturtium, Parsley,
Fennel and Cress.
When the brew is green
And the stem is sweet,
Lie in the water
And Thrice repeat:

I shall bathe
And I shall be
As green and strong,
Good herbs, as thee;
Draw me favour,
Draw me fame,
Draw bright honour
To my name.

Rise from the water
Thrice empowered;
Wear those virtues
You have conjured.

Valerie Worth, *The Crone's Book of Words*

We often say this simple blessing to our children:

> I see the moon
> And the moon sees me.
> God bless the moon
> And God bless me.
>
> Anon.

Blessings and spells are a little like 'positive thinking'. With spells, the rhythms and the repetition are also important. Spells can be as simple as looking at yourself in the mirror every morning and saying 'I'm getting better every day'. Don't give yourself negative messages or spells as they are destructive. Give yourself positive messages: 'I'm getting healthier every day'.

You might like to try talking to your herbs as you pick them, as they did in ancient times, telling the herbs what you want them to do. This is a favourite:

Ancient Gaelic Incantation for Picking Yarrow

> I will pick the smooth Yarrow that my figure may be sweeter, that my lips may be warmer, that my voice may be gladder. May my voice be like a sunbeam, may my lips be like the juice of the strawberry.

What more could you want from a plant? Now you might like to make up your own incantation. In fact, the old herbalists tell us that if picking any part of the elder tree, you *must* tell the elder fairy, who lives in the tree, for what purpose you are going to use the elder. If you don't do this, you will have one very cranky elder fairy. Not a good thing to have in anyone's garden!

Chilblains

Chilli

An effective Chinese remedy for chilblains is mentioned by Albert Leung.[40] Boil 30 g hot chopped chilli pepper in 2–3 L water for five minutes. Strain and use warm water on the chilblains before the blisters break. As chilli promotes blood supply to the skin, this should be very effective. As chilblains are essentially a reduction in blood supply, make sure you are not wearing tight clothing. Eating a good hot curry could be helpful too. Perhaps you could even try a little diluted chilli sauce on the affected area? Make sure it's not too strong or it might burn. An old remedy for cold feet is to put a chilli in your boot! Do not leave it there very long. Chilli deserves respect! Another old remedy is to soak your feet in a bath with a little lemon juice added. It is important to keep your feet/hands warm. Wear gloves and warm footwear.

My favourite mother-in-law used to get chilblains every winter. I read somewhere that a calcium supplement would stop chilblains. She now starts taking calcium every autumn and gets no chilblains! She is the only member of my family to willingly take my herbal potions and lotions. The rest have to be tied down.

Children and Healing Herbs

Children begin by loving their parents. After a time they judge them. Rarely, if ever, do they forgive them.

Oscar Wilde

Some imagination is needed to convince children to take herbal medicine. Many prepared medicines available in health food shops are preserved in alcohol, which may burn children. Many of these medicines give instructions on the bottle for children's dosage, yet the alcohol is just not suitable for them. Simple herbal teas sweetened with sugar or honey and partly cooled are the safest, simplest way to give herbal remedies to children. Teas such as camomile and peppermint are readily available or can be picked fresh from the garden. I usually make up half a cup of tea with boiling water, wait a minute for the herbs or tea bag to infuse, and then fill the cup with cold water.

Aloe vera is a useful herb for a range of childhood complaints—from sunburn to itchy rashes. However, its gooey look worries children. I tell young children the story of how the American Indians used aloe if they had been wounded fighting cowboys. Sometimes children are happier if they apply the herb themselves. It is good to involve toys like a favourite doll. A teddy bears' tea party, with medicinal tea, might also be a good idea. Tablets can be crushed in a mortar and pestle and a little honey added. Children like doing this themselves. Involve the children in their own healing wherever possible, explaining why you think the medicine is important. If they are really unhappy about it, leave it for a while; you might find they come to you asking to take the medicine later.

Bed wetting

Bed wetting is usually an embarrassment rather than a medical problem. Try giving the child a dessertspoon or two of honey before bedtime.

The theory is that honey attracts and holds water. It certainly should be a popular remedy! Make sure the child goes to the toilet before bedtime and restrict the amount of fluids for several hours before bedtime.

Colic

Try a teaspoon of olive oil on an empty stomach. A weak tea made from dill, camomile, peppermint or fennel can also help. Many chemists still sell, or can order in for you, 'Baby's Friend', an old remedy that includes dill. Dill water was the old remedy for babies with colic:

> Infuse ½ teaspoon dill seeds in a cup of boiling water. When lukewarm, strain, discard seeds and give one teaspoon of the liquid after feeds to alleviate wind.

Constipation

Mix slippery elm powder with honey. Roll up into 'lollies'. Give plenty of liquids after the 'lollies' have been eaten. Slippery elm is as nutritious as porridge. One to two dessertspoons should be adequate for a four year old. Slippery elm provides soft emollient bulk. It is not an irritant laxative. Other foods that are laxative include prune juice or stewed prunes, paw paw, apples (and other foods high in roughage) and dried fruit. A very simple and amazingly effective remedy is a large glass of water taken first thing in the morning. If your child can tolerate water warm, even better. A couple of drops of lemon or lime juice make it more palatable. Make sure lots of liquids are drunk. Don't give diuretic soft drinks like cola. Lemonade or water is preferable. A surprising Chinese remedy is to eat 30 g peanuts, fresh or cooked.[41] Be careful of nuts for children as they can choke on whole nuts. Perhaps pure peanut butter (unsalted) may be better for them. Eat this daily until the condition improves. Thirty grams is probably the adult dose, although it is hard to imagine overdosing on peanuts! This is a simple, agreeable and nutritious remedy well worth a try. Another simple remedy is to eat fresh coconut.

Coughs

Essential oil of thyme in steam or a few drops in a perfume light ring or in a scent pot in the room is helpful for coughs. Thyme is an excellent expectorant. Remember that coughing is usually normal. It is your body trying to get rid of mucus. Cough suppressants are mainly used for dry coughs (i.e. when there is no sputum). Try a tea of lemon thyme and honey. Use a few large sprigs of thyme. Lemon thyme tastes better than cooking thyme and is still a very good antiseptic.

Once, lollies and candies were just convenient and tasty ways of taking herbal medicine. Herbal medicinal candies were called pastilles. They were, of course, excellent for children. We still have the remains of some left in the lolly shop—peppermints, liquorice and a few others. Unfortunately, most confectionery nowadays uses synthetic flavours and thus loses any medicinal value. Here is an old recipe for Horehound Candy:

Horehound Candy[42]

Dutch crushed sugar	4.5 kg
Dried horehound leaves	60 g
Cream of tartar	20 g
Water	2.3 L
Anise-seed flavouring	to taste

Pour the water on the horehound leaves and let it gently simmer till reduced to 1.5 litres; then strain the infusion through muslin and add the liquid to the sugar. Put the pan containing the syrup on the fire, and when at a sharp boil add the cream of tartar. Put the lid on the pan for 5 minutes; then remove it and let the sugar boil to stiff-boil degree. Take the pan off the fire and rub portions of the sugar against the side until it produces a creamy appearance; then add the flavouring. Stir well and pour into square tin frames, previously well oiled.

Cradle Cap

Comfrey ointment or a wash with strong (cooled) comfrey tea, is helpful. So, too, is vitamin E oil applied directly to the scalp or mixed with olive oil.

If cradle cap is severe and persistent, it might be related to some food intolerance such as wheat or cow's milk. See if the condition gets worse when particular foods are eaten or better when particular foods are eliminated from the diet. If the child is being breast fed, the nursing mother must check out her own diet.

Cramps

Both of my daughters sometimes get cramps in their legs at night. Increase calcium-containing foods such as cheese, yoghurt and milk; or supplement with dolomite, bone meal, calcium or calcium lactate tablets. Try crushing the tablets in a mortar and pestle with a spoonful of honey for young children. If dairy products are a problem, try fish with edible bones (sardines, salmon and white bait), soya milk, bok choy, tofu or baked beans. A sudden cramp in the calf can best be relieved by gently stretching the clenched muscles.

Adding salt to the diet can help, should the cramp have been caused by excessive loss of sodium chloride in heavy perspiration. For 'night cramp' vitamin E (300–400 iu daily) and/or bonemeal tablets (four to six tablets before retiring) may be helpful.

Diarrhoea

Children under three **must** see a physician as there is a danger of dehydration. Do not treat diarrhoea as a minor ailment in children. It is one of the top ten killers of Australian children. The problem is dehydration. If the diarrhoea is severe or prolonged, get medical help immediately as the situation can become critical very quickly (within a few hours).

For mild diarrhoea, slippery elm can be used. Slippery elm bark powder gives form and bulk to the stools, 'mopping up' excess fluid. It is essential that lots of liquids are taken to avoid dehydration, even more so if slippery elm is being taken. The first symptoms of dehydration are headaches and thirst. One of the best remedies for mild diarrhoea and dehydration is homemade chicken soup. This replaces some of the salts lost with dehydration. Camomile and mint tea with a little honey is helpful. It is okay for children not to eat, but do be careful that they have adequate fluids. Do not give cola soft drinks (such as pepsi and coke), as these contain lots of caffeine, which is a diuretic, and do not give lemonade or similar soft drinks.

Another simple remedy is carrot soup or pureed carrots.

Rice water is a gentle old country remedy. It is the water left from boiling rice and can be sweetened with honey. It has a soothing and anti-inflammatory effect on the stomach and intestines and the starch may 'gel' the stools.

Eating bananas is also helpful.

Check out food allergies or food intolerance (like gluten sensitivity), if diarrhoea is a continuing problem. Allergies often run in families.

If bowel movements are always watery-diarrhoea, your body could be trying to get rid of foods it cannot tolerate or digest.

Insomnia

Try a glass of water. While it sounds too simple to work, try it first. The simple action of drinking is calming.

Camomile tea can be safely given to children. It is the gentle calming tea given to Beatrix Potter's Peter Rabbit. If you have this story you might like to read it to the child while they are sipping their tea.

A glass of milk may also help as it contains calming chemicals. It is best given warm.

Nappy Rash

Nappy rash responds brilliantly to comfrey ointment. At the first signs of a rash we always used comfrey ointment. Jan and I were once babysitting for a friend. When we changed the baby's nappy we were shocked to see an almost red raw bottom and genitals. It was the worst case of nappy rash we had ever seen. After sponging gently and drying thoroughly, we automatically reached for the comfrey and slathered it all over the rash. This was done at every nappy change. The friend came back a few hours later, chatted with us for a while, then discovered her son needed changing. When she took off his nappy she was amazed. The nappy rash had improved dramatically. She had been treating the rash for weeks with all sorts of remedies with little success and was truly astonished to see how effective the comfrey was. She continued using the comfrey ointment until the rash completely disappeared.

Nightmares

We haven't tried it, but a pillow stuffed with dried wood betony is said to stop nightmares. Collect and dry a goodly amount of wood betony and sew it up into a sachet or pillow. Perhaps you and the child could make this together? The psychological benefit of doing this, with as much positive attitude and fanfare as possible, might allay the nightmares anyway. Wood betony *(Stachys betonica* or *Betonica officinalis)* is a pretty ground cover that is good to grow in your garden anyway.

> It [Betony] is good whether for the man's soul or for his body; it shields him against visions and dreams, and the wort is very wholesome, and thus thou shalt gather it, in the month of August without the use of iron; and when thou hast gathered it, shake the

mold till naught of it cleave thereon, and then dry it in the shade very thoroughly, and with its roots altogether reduce it to dust: then use it and take of it when thou needest.

Apuleius, c.400 AD

Temperature

Pour a cup of hot water over a sprig of fresh yarrow, elder flowers, peppermint or catmint. Sweeten. Cool a little and give to the child to sip. Repeat every four hours. Pick a bunch of any or all of these and steep them in the bath water or tie them in a muslin bag to the tap and let the bath water run through them. A drop of any essential oil of mint (spearmint or peppermint) in the bath is also very cooling. (Don't use more than a drop.) Sponging with diluted vinegar is excellent. Very high temperatures can cause dangerous convulsions in babies and young children and this can be very frightening to parents. Medical aid is essential. Babies and small children, unlike adults, are unable to regulate their own temperature. It is terrifying to see a small child convulse with a raging temperature. The treatment for the fever is to put the child in a tepid bath and use whatever methods necessary to get the temperature down. It is important to ensure that the water is not cold because this can cause shivering and raise the child's temperature even further.

Tummy Upsets

Peppermint tea, or camomile and peppermint taken together, are good for a range of tummy problems. Camomile is anti-inflammatory, while peppermint is settling and antispasmodic. My youngest loves peppermint tea, especially tea with heaps of sweetening. These two herbs are not recognised enough for the power they have to help tummy upsets. They are gentle and easy to use and it would be very difficult to overdose with them.

My doctor told me he was taught in medical school to see sick old and sick young people very quickly. The old because they might die; the young because they might get better quickly! Either way you might lose your fee! The point is, children can and do recover from illness quite suddenly. Children are also likely to respond to psychological factors (see spells). The mere belief that a medicine will work is very powerful. At the same time, because children can get worse very suddenly, they need to be watched closely.

Cholesterol Lowering

Plantain

The herb, Greater plantain, has been shown in recent research to lower cholesterol levels significantly. Plantain seed is usually recommended for constipation. Metamucil is psyllum manufactured from plantain by Searle and available from chemists. The seed is also available in health food shops. (The dose of Metamucil used in cholesterol-lowering research was 9–10 g per day for eight weeks.)

Plantain may even help alleviate haemorrhoids.

Garlic

Garlic oil has been shown in modern research to lower cholesterol levels. Fresh garlic cloves can significantly reduce the risk of heart disease generally. This is hardly news to the old herbalists. Dioscorides, writing in the first century AD, tells us:

> It doth cleare the arteries, and being eaten raw or sod, it doth assuage old coughes.

A 17th century translation from the Ancient Greek[43]

Ginseng

Ginseng is another herb useful in treating high cholesterol levels. Use small amounts (1–3 g) daily over a long period if you have high blood pressure (it can elevate blood pressure). If you have normal blood pressure you can take as much as you can afford. It is a very expensive herb. While modern scientists might still disagree over its benefits, racehorse owners have already made their decision about its 'tonic' effects. It is sold by the health food shop next door to the NSW Rosehill racecourse by the truckload!

Guar gum

Guar gum comes attached to the seed pod of the Indian cluster bean (*Cyamopsis tetragonolobus* or *psoralioides*). It grows in tropical Asia, India and Pakistan. The gum is used extensively as a thickening agent in foods and some medicine. In recent research guar gum has been shown to reduce low density lipoprotein cholesterol (the 'bad' cholesterol) levels by 10% to 25% over a three-month period.[44] Amounts from 3 g to 15 g per day have been used. Guar gum seems to encourage the production of bile by the liver. Guar gum should always be taken with large amounts of liquid as it swells to form bulk in the intestine. Because of this it produces a feeling of fullness and has been used in some weight loss formulations.

As guar gum affects blood sugar levels, diabetics should take it under medical supervision.

> Guar gum has been found to reduce post-prandial insulin and glucose levels and appears to be a useful adjunct in the management of non-insulin-dependent diabetes mellitus.[45]

Ginger

Still another herb that has been shown in tests on animals to lower cholesterol is ginger. Ginger not only helped prevent cholesterol absorption but also had a tonic effect on the heart muscle (of guinea pigs).[46,47] So feed yourself and your guinea pig on it!

Fenugreek Seeds

Fenugreek seeds also reduce cholesterol. In rats fed 50% of their diet as fenugreek seeds, cholesterol levels dropped by 58%. Eating this much of any plant is a bit extreme (if not foolhardy), but if you have cholesterol problems the inclusion of some of these herbs with a low-fat diet will be helpful.

Liquorice

Liquorice also lowers blood cholesterol. Do not use the liquorice lolly, but real liquorice. The candy is now made from synthetic anise flavour. You can sometimes buy Italian liquorice juice in solid sticks. As this is very concentrated, don't overdo it.

> The following effects of Liquorice have been verified by modern scientific research: it reduces blood cholesterol, fevers, and inflammation; promotes wound healing; increases bile secretion; decreases gastric secretion; increases blood sodium but decreases blood potassium; and promotes estrus. Liquorice has also been shown to be anti-tussive, anti-ulcer, anti-allergic, and to inhibit the growth of experimentally grown tumours.[48]

This 1984 quote from Albert Leung is interesting to compare with Gerard's 1633 comments on liquorice:

> The root of Liquorice is good against the rough harshness of the throat and brest; it openeth the pipes of the lungs when they be stuffed or stopped, and ripeneth the cough, and bringeth forth flegme.

Dioscorides and Pliny also report that liquorice is good for the stomach and ulcers of the mouth.[49]

Onions

Confirmed by modern research, onions are another old remedy for the heart. High density lipoprotein (HDL) is the good blood cholesterol that acts as a scavenger in the blood, cleaning out the LDL (bad type cholesterol) and taking it to the liver where it is destroyed. HDLs have been shown to increase by up to thirty per cent with 50 g of raw onion taken daily. In tests, onions did not lower total blood cholesterol but 'they triggered shifts in the ratio of good to bad cholesterol, replacing a substantial amount of the destructive LDL (bad type cholesterol) with heart protective HDL cholesterol'.[50]

Other Foods

The following list is a good guide to foods that help reduce LDL cholesterol: oat bran, oatmeal, kidney beans, pinto beans, grapefruit (segments and membrane, not the juice), oranges, apples, yoghurt, barley, eggplant, artichoke, shiitake mushrooms, olive oil, seafood (especially fish oil), strawberries, pineapples, paw paw, bananas, and vitamins B, C and E. Foods with soluble fibre have been shown to reduce cholesterol significantly. One cup of oat bran taken daily by men with high cholesterol levels reduced their readings by twenty per cent. It seems soluble fibre and cholesterol bind together and are eliminated from the body.[51] It certainly looks like a high roughage diet is the way to go.

Colds

(See also Coughs, Temperature)

Scatter a few drops of The Fragrant Garden Breathe Easy Oil, or peppermint, lavender or eucalyptus oil in the bath and in the sick room every few hours. This will help get rid of phlegm, making breathing easier, and killing airborne bacteria. Alternatively, simmer the oils in boiling water or use them in a humidifier or in a light ring.

Chicken Soup

Chicken soup is an old remedy from the Chinese who use the silky or black-fleshed chicken. Recently *The Lawrence Review of Natural Products*, a most erudite scientific review, had this to say about chicken soup:

> Chicken soup has a historical legacy that spans hundreds of generations. It appears to be an effective adjunct in the treatment of mild upper respiratory tract infections.[52]

In other words, it is good for colds. Chicken soup and other hot fluids such as herb teas help the body get rid of phlegm. Yet another good scientific journal says the same thing, with typical scientific tentativeness:[53]

> There is some evidence to suggest that hot aromatic fluids, such as chicken soup, do in fact increase mucociliary clearance.

Composition Powder (for grown-ups only)

There is one old-time remedy that I have personally found a sure-fire cure for colds. It must be taken at the very first signs of a cold, the very first tickle in the throat. Once the cold has taken hold, it is a lot less effective, but composition powder will stop a cold from taking hold. Unfortunately, as its major ingredient is cayenne pepper, it stops a few people in their tracks too! It is an old, old remedy and was often prescribed by the old bush 'doctors' for everything from colds to broken legs! There are many variations on the recipe.

Thompson's Original Recipe for Composition Powder—1833[54]

Take two pounds [900 g] of the Bayberry root bark, one pound [450 g] of the inner bark of Hemlock, one pound [450 g] of Ginger, two ounces [60 g] of Cayenne, two ounces [60 g] of Cloves all pounded fine, sifted through a fine sieve and well mixed together. For a dose take a teaspoonful of this powder, with an equal quantity of sugar and put to it half a tea-cupful of boiling water; to be taken as soon as sufficiently cool, the patient being in bed, or by the fire, covered with a blanket. This ... is a medicine of much value, and may be safely used in all complaints of male or female.

Another Recipe, from Jethro Kloss[55]

Bayberry Bark	8 oz [225 g]
African Ginger	4 oz [113 g]
Prickly Ash Berries	1 oz [30 g]
Canada Snake Root	3 oz [85 g]
African Cayenne	2 drachms [14 g]

A Simpler Recipe[56]

Bayberry Bark (powdered)	1 ounce [30 g]
Wild Ginger	½ oz [15 g]
Cayenne	1 drachm [7 g]

This is more like the composition powder used by the early Australian herbalists and the one that I use. It probably works because no self respecting virus would be seen within miles of such a combination!

Cold Sores

Cold sores are viral infections (herpes simplex virus) that form reddish burning blisters on the lips. They are harmless, will often go away of their own accord, but most people find them unsightly and very unpleasant. They can be triggered by stresses to the immune system (see) such as emotional stress, fever, infections, menstruation and immunosuppressive drugs. Sometimes exposure to the sun can trigger cold sores. If you find this to be the case, wear a sun screen.

Solanum nigrum

One of the most amazing remedies for cold sores is *Solanum nigrum* ointment (freshly made from the fresh herb if possible). Blackberry nightshade *(Solanum nigrum)* is a common garden weed. A simple ointment can be made by infusing 300 g of the chopped herb with 1 L of olive oil. Leave for a few days before using. It seems to be very, very effective. Use the ointment at the very first twinge or itch and continue to apply for a couple of days to ensure that no cold sore develops.

Liquorice

A gel containing liquorice (Herplic) has been used for both oral and genital herpes.[57] The gel has been found to minimise the severity and length of outbreak of herpes.

Other herbal remedies

Other herbal remedies rely generally on their antiseptic and anti-viral effect. These include tincture of myrrh, tincture of calendula, pure lemon juice, tea tree essential oil (neat), lavender essential oil (neat) and bergamot essential oil (neat). Take care as some brands of bergamot oil can make the skin photosensitive and thus promote sunburn. Dab a few drops of any of these onto the cold sore three to four times a day. They can work if you act early enough. Essential oils are very strong bactericides and can kill viruses if they come into contact with them.

Diet

An Irish remedy is to add lots of unsalted baked potato to the diet. Including yoghurt in the diet is also said to be helpful.

All 'immune system help' herbs *(see immune system)* can assist too.

Constipation

What rhubarb, senna, or what purgative drug
Would scour these English hence?
Hear'st thou of them?

Shakespeare, *Macbeth* Act V, Scene III

Rhubarb, senna (tea), figs, mulberries, pine nuts, coconut, banana, apricots and plums are all plants that have been traditionally used for constipation. I prefer to use the herbs that encourage the natural processes such as psyllum and slippery elm rather than irritant herbs such as senna and other purgatives. *(See also Diverticulitis and Children—Constipation.)*

Psyllum seeds are an excellent bulk laxative. The seeds come from the common urban weed, *Plantago major* or greater plantain. You can collect your own fresh seeds, chew them and eat them. Plantain seeds have very little flavour. You can buy them in capsules from the health food shop, or sachets from the chemist (Metamucil). The usual dose is 5–15 g of seed or 0.5–2 g of husk.

Plantain must be taken with plenty of water as it swells and produces

a soft, soothing, mucilaginous mass in the stomach. Drinking water is very important, otherwise plantain can exacerbate constipation. (In fact, water by itself is often a good remedy for constipation.) As well as helping constipation, *Plantago* seeds also provide the bonus of helping haemorrhoids and reducing cholesterol levels. There has been one case reported of an allergic reaction to the pollen of plantain.

Slippery elm is a tree used by American Indians. Slippery elm bark swells in the gut, providing a soothing bulk that encourages peristalsis (movement). It is probably about the best and safest laxative around, safe for people of all ages. As it is about as nutritious as porridge, it can be given to invalids as a food. Try mixing a dessertspoonful with fruit juice and try to eat at least three dessertspoonfuls a day. The best and cheapest way to buy slippery elm is as a fine powder. It is also available in capsule or tablet form but I don't feel these are as good as the powder and you have to take too many.

Corns

At the end of a live two-hour radio program, when I had fended off hundreds of questions about herbs, the last caller asked for a remedy for corns. I could not think of one. Since then, still smarting at my failure, I have gathered lots of remedies, as yet untried (no-one I know has corns). Please let me know if you have success with one of these remedies.

• Dandelion and greater celandine can be used for corns (see also warts). Place sap from the plants on the corn daily.
• A drop of wintergreen oil daily rubbed into the corn is an old remedy.
• A Chinese remedy recommended by Albert Leung involves a bulb of garlic and a green onion. Mash into a paste, place a small amount on the corn and secure with a band-aid. Change every two days. Discontinue if irritation occurs and do not use for more than five applications.[58]
• Lemon juice can be placed neat on the corn night and morning, or paint with turpentine, cover with a bandage and renew every 24 hours.
• Hollow out a swede, fill with salt to draw the liquid out, leave it for 24 hours and then bathe the corn with the liquid night and morning.[59]
• Onions often feature in corn cures. One recipe calls for one baked onion and an equal amount of soft soap. These two are blended or pulped, placed onto a piece of linen and applied to the corn.

- Tape a moist tea bag to a corn for 30 minutes every day and the corn should be gone in a week or two.
- Rub castor oil on the corn twice a day and it will gradually peel off, leaving soft smooth skin.[60]
- Every night, put one piece of fresh lemon peel or pineapple peel on the corn. (The inside of the peel on the outside of the corn.) Do this for at least a week.[61]

Coughs

Coughing in a shady grove
Sat my Juliana.
Lozenges I gave my love,
Ipecacuanha—
Full twenty from the lozenge box
The greedy nymph did pick;
Then sighing sadly, said to me
My Daman, I am sick.

George Canning

A multitude of herbs may help coughs. Take these helpful herbs any way you can—in teas, in cooking or in tablet form: fenugreek seeds, thyme, horseradish, sage, liquorice, comfrey and coltsfoot flowers. Make a tea of any (or all!) of the above herbs using about a teaspoon of dried or two of fresh herb to the cup. These can be taken as necessary— every hour if the cough is severe.

Grandma often infused cough herbs such as the ones above in brandy or 'Bundy' rum. It was certainly a lot easier to talk Grandpa into taking them that way! Alcohol is a good preservative of the medicinal properties of herbs and a 'medicinal brew' will keep for a year or two.

Thyme is an excellent antiseptic expectorant (makes the phlegm come up); a few drops of the essential oil in a vaporiser, bath or steam inhalation is helpful.

Onions are also an old cough remedy. Slice an onion or two and sprinkle the slices with sugar. Leave for an hour or two then collect the sweet onion juice. This is a great cough syrup. If you prefer, mix two or three large chopped or sliced onions with a jar (two cups) of honey. Leave this for a day, then strain the honey syrup. If you wish you can add a splash of brandy or other spirit to this remedy (for reluctant patients).

Cystitis

A bath with a little lavender or sandalwood essential oil—three to six drops to a bath—is helpful. Do this daily. Use less oil if there is burning or irritation.

Sandalwood essential oil is also a urinary tract disinfectant. Wear a few drops regularly as a perfume if you frequently suffer from urinary tract problems. Research has shown that within 30 minutes of putting sandalwood essential oil on the skin it can be found in the urinary tract acting as an antiseptic. Sandalwood is thus a perfume and a medicine in one! Do not use perfume or craft oils, only the natural essential oil of sandalwood.

Cider vinegar in the bath, or used as a douche, is also helpful.

If cystitis is severe or persistent, you should see your medical practitioner for antibiotics, because uncontrolled urinary tract infections can cause kidney damage.

Cyst—see Sebaceous Cyst

Dandruff

Rosemary or nutmeg essential oil rubbed into the scalp is effective for many dandruff sufferers. These oils stimulate blood supply to the scalp and kill all bacteria and fungi. You can add six to ten drops of rosemary oil to your shampoo or conditioner. Rosemary essential oil is antiseptic, antifungal and promotes blood supply to the scalp. *(See also Baldness.)*

Unfortunately, the closest most commercial rosemary shampoos get to rosemary is the picture on the label, so it is best to add your own. Only small amounts are needed (1% or so). More than this can irritate the eyes, although it won't harm them. (If you do get pure essential oil in your eyes, the best first aid treatment is to wash eyes with olive oil rather than water.)

Dandruff is sometimes helped by a zinc supplement or by including in your diet more foods high in zinc, such as oysters, beef and crab. Shampoos with zinc (there are a number of good ones at the chemist) can also help.

Food allergies can promote dandruff in some people, so watch your diet and see if there is any correlation between what you have eaten in the last 48 hours and the severity of your dandruff. The body's levels of zinc can be depleted by chronic infections, alcoholism, surgery, burns or multiple injuries.

Try increasing the quantity of cold-pressed virgin olive oil in your diet and see if this helps.

Depression

Depression is the most common mental problem in the United States ... There are countless reasons to feel despondent and despairing. Some of them are nuclear war, inflation, the Mideast, the Midwest, ageing, death, punk rock ... Only when everything in life is going perfectly is depression a sign of mental illness. If you are depressed, try this quick and easy test to tell if you are crazy.
1. Is your job a delight?
2. Are you lucky in love?
3. Do you have enough money?
If you answered Yes to all three questions, something is seriously wrong with you whether or not you are depressed. If you answered No to any of them you have every reason to be depressed.

James Gormon, *First Aid for Hypochondriacs*

The classic herbs used for depression are saffron, borage, clary sage and nutmeg. B group vitamins are also important.

Saffron *(Crocus sativus)*

The Chinese believe that long-term use of saffron will help depression; not the yellow colouring sometimes sold as saffron, but the dried stigmas of the saffron crocus. As even tiny amounts are quite expensive, synthetic 'sunset yellow' colouring usually replaces it. Add small pieces of real saffron to boiled rice, paella or bouillabaisse. In Cornwall saffron cakes are traditional. Chinese herbalists prescribe it for depression, tightness of the chest and emotional disturbance. If you're feeling miserable, buy some saffron and always include a little in your boiled rice.

Large amounts of saffron should not be used by pregnant women as it is said to have a stimulating effect on the uterus and may cause miscarriage.[62]

Borage

Borage can be taken in salads. Rub the fresh leaves between two tea towels to remove the hairy prickles. Infused in wine or alcoholic drinks, borage improves the flavour of old 'over-the-hill' red wine. Borage contains very large amounts of potassium and wine probably makes it easier for the body to assimilate this potassium.

> The leaf of the Borage hath an excellent spirit to repress the fuliginous vapours of dusky melancholy and so cure madness. It will make a sovereign drink for melancholy passions.
>
> Francis, Lord Bacon.

Lemon Herbs and Oats

Fresh lemon balm tea is cheering and helpful if taken regularly. Try replacing some coffee or tea with fresh lemon balm tea. It is a delicious drink. I find lemon verbena tea cheering too.

Another old remedy for depression is oats, the common breakfast variety.

Nutmeg and Clary Sage

Add a few drops of clary sage essential oil, and/or nutmeg essential oil to the bath. Both these herbs have a reputation for cheering one up. Nutmeg oil has to be one of my favourite oils—its fragrance is just great: deep and spicy yet fresh and clean at the same time.

Vitamin B Deficiency

A deficiency of Vitamin B can cause many health problems, including mood and personality changes. In 1979 the Australian National Health and Medical Research Council found that one in five Australians had an inadequate thiamine level. Alcohol reduces the amount of thiamine in the body.

When I worked as a nurse on a New Year's Eve night shift once, we greeted the battered morning shift with the multi-Bs and the Alka-Seltzer. Very large doses of vitamin B were the medical staff's cure for self-inflicted pain.

Depression is a normal reaction to loss. Where there is no real reason for the depression and it comes upon you suddenly, you may have some chemical imbalance in your body. People who suffer frequently from bouts of black, inconsolable depression, for no obvious reason, are sick and need medical help. This sort of depression is very different from what most of us know as depression. We can often 'jolly' ourselves out of a depressed mood; clinically depressed people can't. It is a pity we use the same word as the difference is much more than one of degree.

Severe depression can be caused by food intolerances, stress, chemicals, hormone imbalance, immune system disorders, malabsorption, gut problems, tumours, coeliac disease, alcohol abuse and vitamin deficiencies—to mention only a few. Get all these checked out by a competent physician (or physicians). Don't blame yourself for your depression. Remember, it is very likely to be caused by a chemical imbalance in your body. No single therapy, or therapist, has all the answers. Seek help from a number of healing professionals. Everything from psychotherapy to massage can be helpful. In the meantime, keep eating your saffron rice.

Diarrhoea in Adults

(See also Children: Diarrhoea)

Slippery Elm

Strangely, slippery elm powder can be used for diarrhoea as well as constipation. It is an excellent, safe and nutritious remedy, albeit a little difficult to get down. Try slippery elm powder for mild diarrhoea. Mix one dessertspoon, thoroughly, in fruit juice and take about three times a day or as necessary.

Blueberries

Blueberries have been used as a traditional remedy in Sweden. Five to ten grams of dried blueberries are made into a soup and given to children. Ironically, though, fresh blueberries can be a laxative for some people.

Blackcurrants are also used to treat diarrhoea. A drug called pecarin is now sold and exported from Sweden as an anti-diarrhoeal drug. The drug is made from the skins of blackcurrants. Both berries contain 'anthrocynosides' which kill the bacteria that often cause diarrhoea.[63]

Plenty of fluids should be taken to prevent dehydration.

Further Suggestions

Where diarrhoea is chronic, check out the possibility of food allergies, lactose intolerance, coeliac disease, colitis or diverticulitis.

High doses of vitamin C can cause diarrhoea. If you are taking high doses of this vitamin, reduce the quantity you are taking. A change in diet and/or a high intake of fruits such as figs, rhubarb and dried fruit can also cause diarrhoea.

Diuretic Herbs

Diuretic herbs increase the flow of urine. If you think you retain too much fluid, get your health professional to check out your heart and kidneys before self-medicating. Diuretics should not be used for weight loss. The loss is only temporary and diuretics put unnecessary strain on the kidneys.

Plants with a diuretic effect include dandelion leaves (young leaves are collected in Italy in summer and added to summer salads—they are highly nutritious); dandelion roots, which are roasted and made into coffee; parsley; tea, coffee and cola drinks (because of their caffeine content); cucumber; kava kava; lemon juice; celery seed; juniper berries (including gin, made from juniper berries); and asparagus. A low-salt diet is also helpful.

Diverticulitis

Diverticulitis is the inflammation of small pouches in the wall of the large bowel. A lot of our older customers have this complaint and have cured it completely or found incredible relief by including slippery elm powder in their diet. At least two dessertspoonfuls of fine-grade powder should be taken with every meal. Try mixing some with fruit juice and drinking it before it sets into a gel. For best results drink lots of water when you are taking slippery elm.

Other mucilage-containing herbs, such as comfrey, should also help. Steep a large, cut up, fresh leaf of comfrey in three cups of boiling water and sip this throughout the day. A few young leaves of comfrey can be chopped and mixed in salads. Small amounts of comfrey are quite safe and promote healing.

> Slippery Elm: an important medicine, as well as food, of the American Indians and pioneers. It is still listed among recognised official drugs, and still considered one of our best emollient and demulcent medicines. It is a valuable article of diet because of its soothing influence upon the stomach and the intestines.[64]

Ears

Do not poke anything into the ear to try to remove something as it might force the foreign body in further. The smallest thing you should pick your ears with is your elbow.

Ringing

Tinnitus, ringing in the ears, can arise from almost any disorder of the ear, from a cold to a blockage. I feel it can sometimes be caused by food or chemical allergies. My ears start to ring shortly after drinking tap water. This could be a sensitivity to chlorine or some other chemical in the water. If you think allergies might be a problem, consult a specialist doctor or naturopath, especially if you have other allergy symptoms.

Wax

Try washing the ears with a little hydrogen peroxide. Leave it to bubble away in your ear for a while until it loosens the wax. A few doses of peroxide can remove all but the most stubborn wax. Warmed olive oil can also soften wax.

Bugs

Bugs are attracted to the light, so shine a torch in the ear or turn the ear toward the sun! If this doesn't work, try lying on your side, gently pull the ear lobe backward and upward to straighten the ear lobe and ear canal. Then float the bug out with warm olive oil or warm water.

Aeroplane Ear

Changes in air pressure as a plane takes off or lands can cause severe ear pain, especially if there is sinus congestion. Avoid travelling if you have a cold or if a child has a runny nose. If this is not possible, try to clear the airways by putting five to ten drops of The Fragrant Garden Breathe Easy Oil on a tissue and breathing in the fumes from this for an hour before takeoff, and during takeoff and landing. Keep blowing the nose to remove as much mucus as possible. Don't let children swallow the mucus; insist that they blow their noses. (If they keep swallowing mucus they are more likely to be airsick too.) Other essential oils that can be used to inhale include eucalyptus or tea tree.

Try to swallow as the plane descends. Give children lollies; give babies the breast or bottle.

Try blowing through your nose while pinching your nostrils closed. Avoid mucus-producing foods like milk products, sweets, chocolate, sugary carbohydrates and alcohol for three days before travelling and avoid these foods during the flight.

Eat mucus-cleansing foods like garlic, onions, vegetables, carrot juice and lots of fresh water. Try a steam inhalation before travelling if you know you are congested.

Earache

Warm an egg-cup full of castor or olive oil. Mix in six to ten drops of an essential oil such as lavender or basil. Place several drops in the ear every hour. Ear infections should be treated seriously as they can cause permanent hearing loss if not treated properly. Serious infections will probably need fast-acting antibiotics, prescribed by a physician.

Take antibiotic herbs such as garlic. If there is nasal congestion as well, a long (20 to 30 minutes) steam inhalation of eucalyptus or tea tree or The Fragrant Garden Breathe Easy Oil can be helpful. Put six to ten drops of any of these oils in boiling water; cover your head and the bowl with a towel and breathe in the medicated vapours. Quite often the infection spreads from the ears to the sinuses (these are located on either side of and above the nose) and to the back of the throat. The combination of steam and essential oil is about the best anti-bacterial or antibiotic you can get. Thirty minutes' inhalation will kill most bugs.

A few drops of essential oil of lavender can also be rubbed behind the ear. This is sometimes helpful for earache.

Persistent earaches, especially in children, should be checked medically. Often antibiotics from your medical practitioner are the best, safest and quickest solution.

Feet

(See also Athlete's Foot and Corns)

Bathe sore feet in warm water with six to eight drops of lavender oil and four drops of armoise (mugwort) oil. If you have it, add some comfrey root or leaf to the water.

We had a middle-aged customer who joined a golf club. The aged members could rarely do more than a few holes before they complained of being tired, and retired. Our customer introduced the club to mugwort. All the old books say that one can walk for miles and never get tired feet if a leaf of mugwort is placed in the shoe. The transformation was astounding with all the elderly gentlemen doing nine to eighteen holes!

There are at least two types of mugwort, one tall (3–4 m) and fragrant, the other short and not fragrant. Which one works best? We don't know—perhaps both. Golfers will just have to experiment and let me know!

A couple of drops of mugwort oil added to your shoe might be worth trying too. Try a few drops of spearmint or peppermint essential oils in a footbath. They are both very cooling and refreshing for feet.

The old trick of transferring your feet from hot water to cold and then back again is also worth a try.

Fevers

(See also Children: Temperature)

A sprig of yarrow *(Achillea millefolium)* or feverfew *(Chrysanthemum parthenium)* in a cup of hot water will help reduce temperature. As yarrow is virtually tasteless it can be given to children with honey. Feverfew has a bitter flavour.

A tepid bath with a drop or two of peppermint oil will also help bring down temperature quickly. Be careful not to use too much peppermint oil as it can be irritating to the skin. A tea of feverfew, as its name implies, will also help. Steep four to eight leaves in a cup of hot water.

Mugwort (armoise) oil and camomile oil both contain azuline, which helps bring down body temperature. Camomile is a safe oil to use around children. Place a few drops in a tepid bath. If no oil is available, one to three camomile tea bags can be placed in the bath, or tie the bags to the hot water tap and let the hot water run through them.

Meadowsweet and White Willow Bark (the original inspiration for aspirin) will also bring down temperature. They contain aspirin-like chemicals. They can be taken as a tea. Meadowsweet *(Spiraea ulmaria)* is much gentler on the stomach and, in fact, is used by herbalists for stomach problems such as hyperacidity, heartburn and peptic ulcer (complaints for which aspirin could not be used).

A fever is the body's way of killing invading bugs. If I have a fever, I prefer to have a hot bath, rug myself up and go to bed and 'sweat it out' as my grandmother would say. If my daughter gets a fever she becomes delirious, and as a small child, would convulse. I prefer to bring her temperature down as quickly as possible!

Flatulence

> Beans, beans, the musical fruit,
> The more you eat, the more you toot,
> The more you toot, the better you feel,
> So eat your beans with every meal.

This can be very embarrassing and annoying. Men, on average, pass wind fourteen times a day; women eight to ten times a day. It can vary between two and forty times a day! There are a number of herbs that can help. These are usually the tummy herbs such as peppermint, camomile, bitters and other digestives.

Try soaking a tablet, preferably dolomite, but a garlic or a vitamin tablet (not a capsule) can be used, in one to two drops of peppermint oil and/or tea tree oil. Take up to three of these a day.

Dill, peppermint, ginger, fennel, caraway and aniseed are all herbs that help flatulence. They can be included in your diet or taken as fresh or dried teas.

Beans are notorious for producing flatulence. Avoid eating a lot of these, or soak them for a few hours before cooking.

If flatulence persists, don't be embarrassed to seek advice from a medical professional.

And a final word on dill:

Dill

Ye decotion of ye dried haire & of ye seed being drank, draws down milk & assuageth the tormina and inflations, & stops both ye belly & ye vomitings that flot on ye top of ye stomach.

Dioscorides, 1st century AD

Food Allergies

Some years ago I discovered I had some food allergies. I was on holiday and being especially chauvinistic to my long-suffering navigator–wife. I was shaking, tense, angry and over-reacting. My usual excuse for this behaviour was that I was stressed from over working—an excuse I couldn't use after being on holiday for four weeks! It was then we realised that something was amiss. After seven years of herbalists, doctors' tests and my own research, I have discovered that if I eat yeast or MSG my brain goes into a fog. I find it very difficult to concentrate or recall things, especially nouns. A simple meal of fish and fresh barbecued vegetables at a Japanese restaurant put me into 'fairyland' for two days. The barbecued vegetables had been sprinkled over and over again with MSG. The immediate reaction was an increase in pulse rate to the extent that my heart started to pound in my ears. My hearing seemed muffled too.

We know that large doses of MSG and related excitotoxic amino acids can induce brain lesions and associated behavioural and endocrinological defects. We must admit that we do not know what the lower doses do.[65]

If I eat wheat I get a butterfly rash on my face, flaky skin and diarrhoea. I was at a bush tucker tour of the Myall Lakes a little while ago. I forgot to take my own provisions and ate wheat and sausages. I spent Monday with ghastly diarrhoea. I was debilitated and totally exhausted for two days. Interestingly, I met a fellow sufferer on this trip, an executive film producer. While she, too, had a wheat allergy, she put it to good use. About half an hour before she had to go to a male-dominated board meeting to fight for funds or for a particular project, she ate a sandwich. The effect was to make her much more aggressive!

Food allergies, then, affect behaviour, thought processes, personality and energy levels. They are insidious and very hard for most people to accept. We really know very little about where they come from and how to treat them.

You need professional help if you suspect food allergies, but you can help yourself by building up your immune system, your adrenal glands and your intestinal tract (with aids like camomile tea or slippery elm powder).

Fungicides

Most essential oils are strong fungicides, and are therefore effective for a great range of complaints, from tinea and thrush to ringworm and giardia. The oils are, possibly, produced by the plants as their own protection against fungus. Tea tree, lavender and sandalwood are especially good fungicides. Be sure to use essential oils and not perfume concentrates.

Glaucoma

Glaucoma is an eye disorder of middle and later life, in which an increase in pressure inside the eye damages the light receptor cells at the back of the eye. Damage to sight can be permanent. Acute glaucoma, with severe eye pain, needs immediate, emergency medical help. The more chronic glaucoma also needs regular medical supervision. Everyone over 40 should have a regular eye test, as the onset of glaucoma can be gradual and unnoticed, until damage is done. Chronic glaucoma is almost symptomless. Some people notice a slight swelling or pressure in the eye, mild headaches or neuralgia over one or both eyes, and the appearance of a 'halo', or rings of light, seen around lamps at night. More usually, glaucoma is diagnosed when the eyes are tested by a

physician. It is possible that there is an allergy factor involved in causing glaucoma,[66] although the causes are unknown. When glaucoma is diagnosed there are a few herbs that you can include in your diet that may be helpful.

Bilberry

Traditionally bilberry, a European form of blueberry, was used for glaucoma. Pizzorno and Murray say this is because of the blue-red pigment found in all berries.[67] Bilberries are hard to find in Australia, although large delicatessens often have the bilberry jam. As it is likely that blueberries and a number of other berries could be helpful, include some of these in your daily diet.

Rue

Rue is even mentioned in Shakespeare's *Hamlet* for improving eyesight. It contains rutin, which has been shown to reduce the damaging pressure of glaucoma. As rue is a terribly bitter herb to take, it is fortunate that rutin is usually available in health food shops. If you decide to grow fresh rue, it is best in a terracotta pot in a sunny spot. Do not overwater it. I would only recommend a small sprig a day taken as a tea. Be careful. Some people are very allergic to rue, which can cause welts on the skin with contact. The easiest rue to grow is 'Jackmans Blue'.

Bioflavinoids

These are found in most citrus fruits. You can buy vitamin C tablets with added bioflavinoids. Pizzorno and Murray recommend taking massive doses of vitamin C—500 mg for every kilo you weigh.[68] (That's 30 g for the average person, which could become quite expensive, and may also cause diarrhoea.) Very large doses of vitamin supplements should be medically supervised.

Marijuana

This is another traditional, if now illegal, herb used for the treatment of glaucoma. It is very difficult to find any information on the use of this herb for glaucoma, however it is probably best taken as a tea or the fresh green leaves eaten on a daily basis. It would be wonderful to see some research on its use for eye complaints. At present its illegality in most states precludes use. Where it is legal, it is vital to remember it can cause intoxication and users must avoid driving or operating machinery.

Gout

> People wish their enemies dead—but I do not;
> I say give them the gout, give them the stone!
>
> Lady Mary Wortley Montague, 1689–1762

Gout, or podogra, is an extremely painful inflammatory disease of the joints. It is caused by too much uric acid in the body. The uric acid finds its way into joints, especially the big toe joints, and renders them liable to attacks of gout. In a typical attack, the patient is awakened at night with severe pain in the toe, which soon becomes hot, shiny, swollen and very tender to touch.

Juniper Berry

The classic herb for gout is juniper berry, a diuretic herb. It has been traditionally used in diseases of the kidney and bladder. The diuretic, kidney-stimulant effect of juniper is probably why it has been used for gout as it may help the body eliminate uric acid and empty the bladder. It may only be the diuretic effect of juniper berry that helps gout, but it may also be that it has an antiseptic and tonic effect on the organs of elimination.

The original way of taking juniper berry was in gin (gin was, and mostly is still, made from juniper berries). Gin was, initially, a herbal medicine for gout and arthritis. It was never intended to be used for anything else! As you really should avoid alcohol if you suffer from gout, using a few drops of the essential oil of juniper in a basin of warm water and soaking your foot in it daily might be a better idea. Alternatively, take up to three drops a day (soaked into a vitamin or dolomite tablet is an easy way of getting it down). Avoid prolonged and continuous use of juniper berry as it may damage your kidneys.

Perilla

Perilla is a Japanese herb often found in Japanese pickles. It is an easy-to-grow annual herb that looks a little like basil. James Duke, in his *Handbook of Edible Weeds*, says that Japanese researchers have found a powerful anti-gout chemical in the leaves of perilla. If you suffer from gout it might be worth including some perilla in your diet. See also the remedies suggested for arthritis.

Diet

Gout can also be helped with diet. Avoid food high in uric acid and purine, such as meat, sweetbreads, liver, kidneys, anchovies, wheatgerm and alcohol. Sour cherries, strawberries and celery are said to be helpful for gout. Celery seed is a diuretic kidney stimulant and will help remove uric acid. It can be purchased at health food shops, often mixed with juniper. Meadowsweet is also good for gout. Take it as a tea (3–6 cups a day) or buy it as a tincture or make your own wine by soaking a good handful in alcohol and sip a little every few hours.

And a final suggestion from *The Doctor's Book of Home Remedies*:

> Urinating isn't the only way to get rid of uric acid. One study showed that among men, frequent sexual activity reduces uric acid levels. The study suggests that more sex means less gout—for men anyway.[69]

Haemorrhoids

Haemorrhoids, or 'piles', are varicose veins of the rectal wall, that is, dilated and engorged blood vessels located inside the rectum which sometimes stick out like little bunches of grapes. They are painful and often bleed a lot, though usually they are not painful when they are bleeding.

Pilewort and Comfrey Ointment

These are good first-aid treatments to relieve the pain and discomfort of haemorrhoids. Slather the area with lots of ointment. If necessary, wear a protective pad. While you are applying the ointment, try easing the haemorrhoids back up the rectal passage if this can be done easily.

Horse Chestnut Tea

An old remedy for varicose veins and haemorrhoids. Use one to two teaspoons of horse chestnut fruit and leaves to one cup of hot water. Drink this three times a day. The tea can also be used as a lotion on the haemorrhoids.

Yarrow Tea

A sprig of yarrow to a cup, taken regularly, is an old folk remedy for bleeding haemorrhoids. Certainly yarrow contains substances that stop bleeding, although it is usually applied externally for this purpose.

Many natural therapists recommend a high roughage diet for haemorrhoids. Psyllum-containing medicines, such as Vi-Siblin, may be helpful for haemorrhoids. Hauseman and Hurley quote research that has shown a reduction in anal pain and bleeding within six weeks with psyllum-type products such as Metamucil.[70] Try increasing your roughage for a week or two. It is certainly the easiest way of managing piles. A sachet or two or Metamucil a day may be all that is required.

Regular exercise is recommended too, especially if your job involves sitting at a desk all day.

Slippery Elm

If haemorrhoids are accompanied by constipation, include at least six dessertspoons of slipper elm powder in your daily diet. You may have to adjust your own level of roughage and demulcent and mucilaginous herbs. Whatever you do, be sure to drink daily at least three litres of water if you are taking slippery elm or psyllum.

Vitamins

Some vitamins are helpful for haemorrhoids, especially vitamin E. Take very large doses (at least 1000 IU) daily. Those who are allergic to wheat should take synthetic vitamin E. Other vitamins that are said to help include B_6, C, A, and bioflavonoids.

Ginkgo

Recently, *Ginkgo biloba* has been recommended for varicose veins, so this might be worth a try. Simmer a large leaf in two cups of water; or fill a jar with leaves and alcohol (vodka, brandy) and soak for a week. Take a nip of this infusion daily.

A caffeine-free diet is also helpful i.e. no chocolate, tea, coffee, cola drinks or Yerba maté tea.

Hair, Greying

One of the saddest letters we have ever received contained $2 and asked for help for a child of 12 years whose hair was greying. We didn't know what to say. Here is a collection of remedies and observations from others that might help.

Chris Reading, a Sydney orthomolecular psychiatrist, told me that greying hair was a sign of poor liver function. If that is true, liver herbs such as dandelion and St Mary's thistle should help. St Mary's thistle is such a powerful liver herb that it can stop liver damage caused by eating poisonous mushrooms. Wherever there are suspected liver problems, these herbs should be included in the daily diet. The leaves of dandelion can be included in a salad. They are bitter, but can be blanched or hidden in a salad and smothered with dressing. Dandelion 'coffee' (beverage might be a better word; it is a poor imitation of coffee) is another way of taking dandelion.

Albert Leung gives this Chinese remedy:

> For treating white hair in young people, an old remedy calls for pulling off the white hairs and then rubbing the empty hair follicles with a small amount of honey. The hair is said to grow out to its original dark colour.[71]

Sesame seeds, too, Leung says, have been used in Chinese medicine to treat premature greying of the hair. Just add 10 to 15 g to your daily diet. Interestingly, sesame is also considered by the Chinese to revitalise the liver and kidneys.

The Wilens give this strange recipe which is not only supposed to stop hair greying, but encourage hair growth as well! 'Three times a day, 5 minutes each time, buff your fingernails with your fingernails. In other words, rub the fingernails of your right hand across the fingernails of your left hand.'[72] Well . . .

Sage is the classic herb for greying hair. Use a strong infusion of the leaves or the essential oil. The essential oil of sage can be rubbed directly into the hair (six drops daily) or added to shampoo or conditioner. Leave the sage on the scalp for ten to twenty minutes.

One customer in his late fifties with a shock of wavy black hair swore that he was grey until he started taking dolomite tablets daily. Dolomite is a form of calcium with lots of magnesium. Donald Law says that greying hair is 'indicative of lack of copper in diet and vitamin B deficiency'.[73] If this is true, a copper bracelet and a vitamin B supplement would help. If B vitamins are not being absorbed this might indicate a malabsorption problem, which could be caused by any number of factors including hereditary disorders (coeliac disease), food allergies and/or candida infestation of the gut.

Hangovers

Last evening you were drinking deep,
So now your head aches. Go to sleep;
Take some boiled cabbage when you wake;
And there's an end of your headache.

Alexis[74]

In this age of the breathalyser, hangovers are certainly less ubiquitous than they used to be. Alcohol interferes with absorption of vitamin B. Vitamin B is essential for the outer covering of all nerve fibres (the myelin sheath). Without this protective coating our nerves start to look like frayed electricity wires. Alcoholics develop 'peripheral neuritis' as this sheath is destroyed. Pretty soon everything is starting to short circuit!

Alcohol is also a diuretic. As the headache of a hangover is caused by dehydration, be sure to drink lots of water while drinking alcohol, or before going to bed. Take lots of vitamin B before going out, before going to bed, or first thing in the morning.

A long warm soak in a bath, with six to eight drops of essential oil of rosemary added, is also a help. As excessive alcohol can damage the liver, take some St Mary's thistle tincture or dandelion coffee.

Perhaps the most pleasant remedy for a hangover that I have seen is a Chinese one: simply eat about 150 g of fresh strawberries!

Headache

What's the best way of getting rid of headaches?
Stick your head through an unopened window.
The pane goes.

Bill, the Steam Shovel
Mr Squiggle, ABC Children's Television

Minor

A smear of lavender essential oil rubbed into the temples is a good, simple old remedy for a headache. Use only a drop or two and don't get it in your eyes, as it will irritate. You can repeat this treatment as often as necessary.

The Fragrant Garden Breathe Easy Oil can also be used in the same way. It is especially effective for sinus headaches. Valerian tea is calming and helpful.

White willow bark and meadowsweet are 'herbal aspirins'. A tea of either will help a headache. The botanical name for meadowsweet was *Spiraea ulmaria*, from which we get the name aspirin. But meadowsweet tea is much kinder and gentler on the stomach than aspirin.

A customer who had tried everything else for sinus and its associated headache gets rid of his headache by putting three drops of anise oil on the back of his tongue whenever necessary. Basil essential oil should also do the same job.

Migraine

Feverfew
Chewing three leaves a day of this pretty annual daisy is a preventative in nine out of ten cases of migraine. Some people get mouth ulcers from chewing the fresh herb and so need to take it in drops. Feverfew is available, preserved in alcohol, from health food shops or you can preserve your own fresh leaves in vodka. Simply half-fill a vodka bottle with fresh leaves and then fill the bottle with vodka and let the leaves infuse in the alcohol. As the strength of the home-made tinctures can vary, start with a few drops in water three times a day and increase (or reduce) dosage as you think necessary. Any spirituous alcohol can be used. Arthritis sufferers might like to use gin.

Lemon Balm
Lemon balm tea is helpful for many migraine sufferers. A cup of fresh lemon balm tea taken daily is said to cure 50% of people who chronically suffer from migraine headaches. It is said to be a preventative, like feverfew. The dried herb is not effective. Most lemon herbs do not retain their flavour when dried. It seems they do not retain their medicinal properties either, although in theory a fresh plant tincture such as the one suggested for feverfew should work. Use a sprig or two to a cup of hot water. It is quite a pleasant herbal tea.

Migraine is often a symptom of food allergy, compounded by a hectic and stressful lifestyle. (*See also immune system* as herbs that help the immune system will also help allergies.) Some foods such as chocolate, oranges and strawberries can give some people migraine, even up to 48 hours after they have been eaten. Check out your allergies with your medical adviser.

Fish oils are said to help migraine headaches.

Another cause of headaches

Some so-called migraine headaches have turned out to be severe sinus headaches (*see sinus*).

Hiccoughs

We once had a middle-aged lady ask for a remedy for hiccoughs—she had had them continually since she was 18 years old! We searched through the books on sale in the shop and found a very complex old formula for curing hiccoughs. We sent her to Newton's Pharmacy in Sydney, to have the complicated formula made up. Three weeks later she rang to say she was cured. We were all delighted. Now we have lost the remedy and lost contact with the lady! Perhaps she is reading this?

Here are some of the hiccough remedies we have heard about since then.
- Suck a lump of sugar on which two or three drops of essential oil of peppermint or cinnamon have been dropped.
- Suck a lump of sugar soaked in vinegar.
- Chew some fresh mint leaves.
- Drink a cup of cool camomile tea.
- Swallow a teaspoon of fresh onion juice.
- Drink a glass of fresh pineapple or orange juice.
- Suck a slice of lemon.
- Breathe in and out of a paper bag.

Continual and chronic hiccoughs can be caused by damage to the breathing centre of the brain or inflammation of the phrenic nerve. If the hiccoughs continue for several hours, particularly in an older person, seek medical advice.

Immune System Help

(See also Arthritis and Cancer)

The immune system is the system the body uses to protect itself from disease. When the body is under attack from 'germs', it calls out the immune system troops. The body temperature is raised to burn out the invader. Adrenalin is released into the bloodstream, and all the muscles (including the heart) go on alert, ready to fight. Sugar is released into the bloodstream ready to supply the muscles with extra energy for the fight. Diseases such as allergies, cancer and arthritis are now seen as immune system disorders. For example, in food allergies, the body attacks the food as if it were an invading germ. This is why the symptoms of food allergy include such things as a racing pulse, hyperactivity (from the extra sugar being released) followed by lethargy (as the sugar is used up), elevated temperature and 'malaise'.

A number of herbs and vitamins have been shown to act as a tonic or a help to the immune system. These plants include coneflower *(Echinacea)* and inkweed or pokeroot *(Phytolacca decandra*, or *P. americana)*. The roots of the pretty coneflower (sometimes called Blackeyed Susan) are boiled into a strong tea (decoction). It is a safe herb to use, even for children, and is easy to obtain. If possible, grow your own; it is a very pretty plant. Traditionally, only the roots were used. However, German herbalists now seem to be using the whole plant.

Pokeroot should be taken under supervision, as it can be toxic if not taken, or prepared, correctly. Early American settlers used to infuse the berries in whisky.

Other immunostimulant plants, which I mention out of interest only, are those containing linoleic acid, such as evening primrose (oil) and borage (seed oil). Wagner also lists the following: *Aristolochia clematitis; Eupatorium perfoliatum; Arnica montana; Sabal serulata; Camomilla recutita; Zexmenia brevifolia; Coriolus consors; Stephaniadepharantha;* and mucilage containing herbs such as *Althera officinalis* (marshmallow), *Plantago major* (plantain), and *Symphytum officinale* (comfrey).[75]

> In recent times, a number of plants (including species of Echinacea and Eupatorium as well as Camomile, Calendula, Baptisia, Arnica and Eleuthrococcus among others) have been shown to contain polysaccharide fractions of a relatively high molecular weight which showed significant immunostimulating properties.[76]

Other measures that seem to help the immune system include vitamins A (found in yellow vegetables) and C; seafood, fish and fish oils containing linoleic acid and seaweed.

Immune system disorders include: asthma; allergies; arthritis; systemic lupus erythematosus; probably chronic fatigue syndrome; and

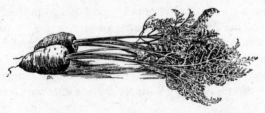

cancer. In fact, many of the major medical problems of the Western world.

Dr Chris Reading has claimed to control a wide range of immune system disorders (including SLE/lupus and AIDS) with massive doses of vitamins, minerals and oils. We still have a lot to learn about the immune system.

Indigestion—see Tummy

Insect bites

Peppermint Oil relieves the pain and irritation of mosquito bites, and Pennyroyal Oil is much used as a remedy and preventative. Camphor, Oil of Cloves, Oil of Cinnamon, and Oils of Rosemary, Eucalyptus, or Cajuput act in the same way as preventatives. Poultices of Ipecacuanha and Mint Leaves relieve mosquito bites.[77]

Aloe vera gel rubbed onto the bite brings almost instant relief. Break open a fresh leaf and place it on the bite. Rub aloe onto the bite frequently if the bite is severe. The yellow sap from under the skin of aloe can stain, however, like the gel, it is very soothing. A drop or two of neat tea tree oil on an insect bite will often take away the irritation and sooth the inflammation.

Insect Repellents

Eucalyptus oil will repel mosquitoes. Rub it over the uncovered areas of your body.[78]

Most insects have amazingly good senses of smell. They can smell a good meal miles away. To repel them you need to confuse them with smell camouflage. Aromatic herbs, of course, are ideal for this. Some herbs work better than others. Some work only with some insects.

Citronella or lavender oil are both good for repelling mosquitoes. Pennyroyal oil repels fleas. Wormwood leaves, rubbed onto clothes or a hat, keep away the flies. The large mugwort, crushed, is helpful against biting insects. The more fragrance you have about, the less insects you will see. Be careful when you rub neat essential oils on your body as they can irritate sensitive skin. Don't get them near your eyes. Candles containing more than ten per cent of natural citronella or lavender oil can often help 'smell camouflage' an outdoor area.

Itches

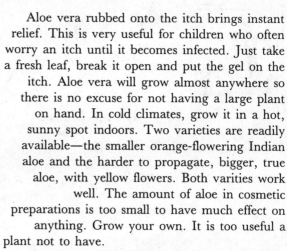

Aloe vera rubbed onto the itch brings instant relief. This is very useful for children who often worry an itch until it becomes infected. Just take a fresh leaf, break it open and put the gel on the itch. Aloe vera will grow almost anywhere so there is no excuse for not having a large plant on hand. In cold climates, grow it in a hot, sunny spot indoors. Two varieties are readily available—the smaller orange-flowering Indian aloe and the harder to propagate, bigger, true aloe, with yellow flowers. Both varities work well. The amount of aloe in cosmetic preparations is too small to have much effect on anything. Grow your own. It is too useful a plant not to have.

Use aloe with chicken pox sores too, to stop the itch. You may need to apply the gel several times, and the earlier in the disease, the better.

Lavender or tea tree oil is also helpful, dabbed neat on itchy insect bites. One or both of these oils should be taken on every camping trip.

Leg ulcers—see Ulcers

Liver Tonic Herbs

The common milk thistle *(Silybum marianum)* is an amazingly effective liver restorative and protective herb. Silymarin, one of the many chemicals in milk thistle, has been shown in recent research with rats to protect the liver from very toxic and life-threatening liver poisons, such as that of the deadly mushroom *Amanita phalloides*. Rats who were given milk thistle lived after eating the poisonous mushrooms, while those who didn't take milk thistle died.[79] It is likely that herbs and vegetables in the milk thistle family, such as globe artichokes, will also be helpful for the liver.

Some people with liver damage caused by hepatitis improved significantly after six to twelve months of taking 420 mg/day of silymarin.

Milk thistle also contains other chemicals that seem to protect the liver from serious biological and chemical damage.

Other herbs that are good for the liver include dandelion and fennel. Dandelion coffee or tincture can be taken safely in large amounts.

> Thistle is a herb of Mars ... It is an excellent remedy against yellow jaundice and other infirmities of the galls, because Mars governs choller.
> Culpeper, 1652.

And three centuries later:

> Milk Thistle extract and its major components have been shown in animal and human studies to exert a hepatoprotectant effect. The compounds reduce liver damage caused by biological and chemical insult. These compounds are being investigated in the treatment of Amanita mushroom poisoning and in the treatment of chronic cirrhosis and appear to offer great promise.[80]
> March, 1988

Living Longer (and well)

Reducing your blood cholesterol levels is the twentieth century charm for living longer. Interestingly, Chinese and Western herbal medicine and alchemy have looked for similar charms for generations. Mainstream Western medicine has in the past been interested more in disease than the maintenance of health. Here are some old and new ways of living longer.

Sage *(Salvia officinalis* and *Salvia purpurea)*

Sage, especially Red Sage, has been recommended by Chinese and English herbalists over the generations for prolonging life. 'He that would eat sage in May, will live for aye' is an old English saying.

Ginseng (*Panex ginseng* or *Panex quinquefolius*)

According to ancient Chinese medicine, ginseng will:

> Vitalise the five organs, calm the nerves, stop palpitation due to fright, brighten vision, increase intellect, and with long term use, prolong life and make one feel young.

Shennong Herbal, 200 BC

Leung says that the usual daily dose is 1.5 to 9 g.[81] Stephen Fulder, in his definitive book on ginseng, *The Root of Being*, says that people under forty should take the herb for one month a year, more than this not being necessary.[82] He says that people over forty should take ginseng daily. (If you have high blood pressure, ginseng should only be taken in small doses.)

Spells (*see also Charms*)

Many psychologists believe that people 'script' or talk themselves into old age and decrepitude. While we have all heard the saying 'You're only as old as you feel', the truth seems to be 'You are as old as you tell yourself you feel'. Louise L. Hay recommends this spell, or what she calls an affirmation, for feeling young, 'I love and accept myself at every age. Each moment in life is perfect.'[83]

While its sentiments are splendid, Louise Hay's spell appears to have lost the power of the 'chant', the rhythmical affirmation that helps us think about what is happening in our head.

Ginseng is a herb that will help you feel younger. It would be even better if you could make up a great rhythmical poem to say while you drink your ginseng tea! For example:

> Ginseng tea, ginseng tea,
> Give the gift of youth to me.

Try writing one for yourself.

Eating Less

Research by Dr Roy Walford seems to indicate that eating a balanced nutritious diet, but much less food, prolongs life (in rats at least).[84] He feels that the easiest way to do this is with a regular fast. Interestingly, many zoos fast to their animals one day a week, as this more closely approximates their life in the wild.

Memory

A herb that we can take to improve our memories! 'This is where the book delves into fairy stories', I hear you say. In fact, two herbs are traditionally used for improving memory—rosemary and sage. Rosemary tea used to be drunk by students to help improve their performance in exams. As rosemary does seem to promote blood supply to the head, this might account for its reputation. Sage tea has a similar reputation and the people who drank sage tea were said to be 'sages' or wise people.

Recently, there has been some interesting research on a very old and beautiful Chinese tree with the unlikely botanical name *Ginkgo biloba*. Ginkgo seems not only to help short-term memory but to slow the ageing process as well. Again, like rosemary, ginkgo seems to increase the supply of blood and oxygen to the brain. Ginkgo helps keep the brain supplied with glucose, its major source of energy.

Ginkgo is particularly beneficial for people who are just beginning to experience deterioration in their cognitive functions. The extract may delay deterioration and enable these subjects to maintain a normal life and escape institutionalization.[85]

All three of these memory herbs are simplicity itself to take; just pour hot water over the leaves and make a memory tea. As most research into ginkgo has used very strong (50:1) extracts, quite a lot of gingko tea would be needed to achieve similar results. However, if you want to plant a tree, you would be hard-pressed to find a prettier deciduous tree. Instead of composting the leaves you can make tea from them and perhaps you'll remember to do the same the following year!

Menstrual Problems

> Then there was the *man* who died of pre-menstrual tension. His wife
> shot him.[86]

Menstrual problems can be many and varied and would probably best
be solved in discussions with your medical practitioner. We could devote
a whole book to the topic. The two classic herbs that are used are sage
and chaste tree.

Chaste Tree Berries *(Vitex agnus castus)* or Monk's Pepper

We had a frantic telephone call from a country customer one day, asking
us to ship up urgently a few chaste trees. It seems her daughter used
to suffer from severe menstrual pain every month. All medical treatment
had been to no avail. Finally a local herbalist put her daughter on a
tincture of chaste tree berries. From that time on she had had no pain.
The government, for reasons of its own, decided to ban the importation
of chaste berries and, without the medicine, her pain had returned.
She now grows her own chaste trees, collects the berries and has no
menstrual pain. The chaste tree influences the hormones, hence its old
medieval name.

> Chasteberry has the effect of stimulating and normalising pituitary
> gland functions, especially its progesterone function. It has, for
> instance, a great reputation as both an aphrodisiac and an
> anaphrodisiac. It will always enable what is appropriate to occur.[87]

To take chasteberries, make a tea using about one teaspoon of ripe
berries to a cup. This can be taken three times a day, but adjust it
according to how you feel. You will have to grow your own trees in
Australia.

Medieval knights on their way to the Crusades knew all about the
chaste tree. It is said that the knights gave chaste tree to their wives
to reduce their libido and keep them 'chaste' while they were away
at the Crusades.

Sage

Sage is also excellent for the hot flushes (or flashes) that are such an
annoying and sometimes very distressing part of menopause. A simple
tea of fresh or dried sage is taken as needed. Use a sprig of fresh herb
to a cup.

Angelica

Angelica is a beautiful, tall herb and is used in China to regulate periods and alleviate cramps and hot flushes. It is sold in capsules as 'Dong-quai' in Chinese herbal shops. Angelica was once candied and used as decoration on cakes or included in mixed dried fruit. Nowadays, strips of green dyed gelatine are used to mimic angelica. It is an easy-to-grow, stately biennial that would grace any herb garden. There is also a stunning dark green form of angelica with very pretty leaves. I don't know if it works just as well. Try it and see!

Chilli (cayenne)

I was doing a television segment on NBN Newcastle's morning program one winter's day on herbs for coughs and colds. Chilli featured prominently. The presenter said she always had at least one hot curry a month as it stopped her period pain. She used to get severe pain, tried hot curry with lashings of chilli about a week before her period was due and, hey presto! no period pain. This surprised me at first but then I thought, well, chilli is warming and certainly promotes blood flow. (Many people ease menstrual pain with a hot bath or hot water bottle, which would also be promoting blood supply). In herbal medicine cayenne (chilli) is seen as a general tonic for the heart, circulatory and digestive systems.

Guelder Rose

The Guelder rose *(Viburnum opulus)* is a commonly grown ornamental in our area. Better known as the Snowball Tree, its old American name is Cramp Bark and it was used for menstrual and other cramps (in the legs) and for spasms. It was once made into tablets and tinctures but these are now not so easy to find. If you have it growing in your garden, scrape a teaspoon of bark off the plant, make a tea with a cup of boiling water and take three or so cups a day.

It is fairly obvious that all these herbs influence hormone levels or prostaglandins in the body. Exactly how, no one seems to know.

Mother's Milk

Too Much

Sage tea is a 'drying' herb. Try a fresh sprig in a cup of hot water and sweetened to taste. Take this tea as often as necessary.

Too Little

Try a tea made by soaking a few fenugreek seeds in a cup of hot water. Fenugreek seeds can be sprouted and eaten in a salad. Fennel, aniseed and raspberries (raspberry leaf is better) are said to help. So too is borage. Add a little chopped borage to a salad and eat half an hour before feeding the baby. Blessed thistle *(Cnicus benedictus)* is a rampant outback weed. Make a strong tea of the plant and drink half an hour before feeding. Often the alcoholic tincture of the plant can be found in health food shops or your local herbalist might have some on his shelves. It is one of the nicer tasting herbal medicines.

Beer or stout is the remedy preferred by the nursing staff at our local hospital.

For excellent advice on feeding babies contact your local Nursing Mothers' Association.

Nail Biting

The old remedy for nail biting was to paint your fingernails with the yellow sap from Aloe vera. Because it tastes so awful, aversion therapy comes into play and eventually you stop biting your fingernails. This is a remedy for the desperate that you should inflict only on yourself, not on others!

Nausea—Morning and Motion Sickness

Seasickness

At first you are so sick you are afraid you will die,
and then you are so sick you are afraid you won't die.

Mark Twain

Herbs for nausea are all quite yummy. Airlines should include them in their catering! The three herbs that are best for nausea are chocolate, peppermint and ginger. We don't know if chocolate-coated peppermints or chocolate-coated ginger works but there must be a lot of pregnant ladies out there who might like to trial them and let me know.

Ginger is so effective in preventing motion sickness that in tests it was shown to be far superior to dramamine, a modern drug for motion sickness. Take about half a teaspoon of ginger powder about 30 minutes before travelling, or put a drop or two of ginger essential oil on a tablet and swallow.

The essential oil of ginger or peppermint can also be placed in an unused car ashtray with a handful of kitty litter or other absorbent material, or you can dab the oil on a handkerchief. Use only a couple of drops. Beware of placing it on plastic or rubber surfaces. Many essential oils can dissolve these surfaces. Essential oils can also damage French polishing and timber finishes.

The Chinese also recommend candied quince as a remedy for morning sickness and motion sickness. This is another pleasant remedy for those who don't like ginger.

Pain Killers

Most pain killers come from herbs. Unfortunately (or fortunately, depending on your point of view), most are illegal or available only on prescription. The opium poppy is the great herbal pain killer, but because of its abuse is not readily available.

Aspirin is commonly found in two plants, the white willow tree and meadowsweet. Meadowsweet can be taken as a tea. It is an easy herb to grow, a common hedgerow weed in England. It has pretty, fragrant, feathery fronds of flowers and likes damp, fertile soil.

Pimples—see Acne

Pregnant

How to become

Golden Seal root

If you have attempted all the time honoured ways of becoming pregnant and checked out all the equipment with the doctor, you might like to try some herbs used by the squaws of the American Indian tribes. These tribal women were among the most intelligent and knowledgeable herbalists around, especially when it came to women's health problems. Modern herbalists claim that Golden Seal root changes the viscosity of the vaginal mucus, making it easier for the sperm to travel to the ova. This treatment is certainly worth a try. Buy a good quality fresh tincture and take as directed on the bottle. Alternatively, take a cup of Golden Seal tea a day. Take for a few months (see also aphrodisiacs). Golden Seal has a (our daughter's words) 'truly disgusting' taste so you need to be keen and persistent.

A valuable member of The Fragrant Garden staff had been trying to get pregnant for some years. After three months on the Golden Seal tincture I had given her she became pregnant and resigned from the job. My wife Jan, while delighted at the success of the Golden Seal, was cranky that she would now have to find a replacement. She announced in an uncharitable tone at a dinner party that I had managed to get one of her best staff members pregnant and now she would have to find someone else! It took some time to get people's jaws back off the ground.

True Unicorn Root

Another herb that others have tried with success is True Unicorn Root. Both Golden Seal and Unicorn Root can be purchased as tinctures (alcoholic extract) from a herbalist or naturopathic chemist. They are not readily available and are probably best taken under the supervision of a good herbalist.

Aloe vera

James Duke quotes some interesting research on aloe.

> Without commenting on the contradiction Rama noted fertility and profertility reports. Alcoholic and water extracts showed 85% reduction in fertility with experimental rats. But one compound with aloe as the main ingredient was useful in cases of infertility associated with irregular menstrual cycles. The same compound improved the fertility of patients with functional sterility and improved their menstrual functions.[88]

Obviously, more work needs to be done but it seems Aloe vera may promote fertility where that infertility is caused by disturbed menstrual function. Include some in your diet if you fall into this category.

How not to become

The contraceptive pill was developed from sweet potato-like yams; it might be advisable to avoid these if infertility is a problem, but the research is inconclusive. Other foods that might adversely influence conception include soybeans, peas and other legumes. Most legumes are rich in natural estrogens, which might possibly act as natural contraceptives. Jean Carper maintains that the population of Tibet has remained stationary for the last 200 years and that their staple diet consists of barley and peas. How on earth do vegetarians ever get pregnant?

Crude Cotton Seed Oil

Crude cotton seed oil, which is used as a cooking oil, contains gossypol, a very potent (efficacy of 99.07%) male anti-fertility agent. It may also interfere with female fertility. Gossypol is also found in the stem and root of the cotton plant. Clinical tests on a male 'pill' are now well under way in China using various levels of gossypol and studying its side effects, which seem very few at this stage. Gerard, writing some four hundred years ago, seems to disagree:

> The seed of cottons tireth up the lust of the body by increasing natural seed, wherefore it surpasseth.[89]

Marijuana *(Cannabis sativa)*

Research by Lewis and Elvin Lewis suggests that marijuana may cause impotence and temporary sterility in men.[90]

Turmeric

In a recent study in China, extracts of the spice turmeric, were shown to be 100% effective in preventing pregnancy in female rats.[91] Turmeric is a spice commonly used in curries.

Orange blossom

At a conference recently, Gregory A'Kent, the Australian naturopath, told me that the United Nations had found that the common garden shrub *Murraya paniculata* (Mexican orange blossom) was an effective 'morning-after' pill. Apparently a simple tea made from a sprig of this bush in hot water the morning after intercourse can prevent pregnancy.

Rheumatism—see Arthritis

Ringworm

When Jan returned from a trip to China, she had a strange mark on her stomach, the like of which I'd never seen. When she went to the doctor, he laughed and said, 'Michael can treat that for you. It's ringworm.' And after several applications of Essential Oil of Lavender, the ringworm completely disappeared.

Ringworm is not a worm, but a fungal infection of the skin or nails. It can be easily eliminated with liberal applications of essential oils such as lavender or tea tree. Tea tree oil is an excellent fungicide. Lavender oil is not as strong but it is gentler on sensitive skin. Apply several drops of either oil to cotton wool or lint and bandage to infection; replace every two to three hours. If skin irritation occurs, dilute essential oil with olive oil. The infection should clear up within a few days.

Sebaceous Cyst

Sebaceous (grease) glands in the skin can become blocked. The continuing production of grease causes the blocked gland to swell into a cyst, which bulges above the surface of the skin. The size of a pea when first noticed, it can grow to that of a golfball. Check with your GP that it is not cancerous. If it is not, it can be very easily removed with comfrey ointment. Comfrey ointment draws and opens up a cyst. Put lots of ointment on a gauze bandage and put this on the cyst daily until the cyst bursts (four to seven days). It is important to allow the cyst to drain at this point. If you keep using the comfrey it may heal over again. Bandage with a sterile dressing and a little antiseptic ointment or calendula ointment until healing is complete.

Shingles

Shingles *(Herpes zoster)* is caused by the same virus as chickenpox. It causes a 'belt' of small blisters around the body and is very painful. The pain is often felt for several days before the rash appears. Many of my customers have found that fresh Aloe vera leaves applied to the rash are a stunningly successful remedy for shingles. I have no idea why this should work, but scores of people have found great relief. Just break open a fresh aloe leaf and apply as much and as often as necessary. Herb pain killers can also be taken.

The virus is contained in the blisters, so contaminated dressings should be burnt.

Sinusitis

There are sinuses on each side of the head. They are small 'holes' or cavities. When these become congested with phlegm and mucus they can be a real misery. The lining of the sinuses on the forehead can swell and cause headaches. The mucus from sinuses can also flow down the throat, causing catarrh and sore throats. The sinuses can also become infected, resulting in sinusitis.

Often, however, sinus problems cause a range of vague symptoms such as malaise, 'woolly head' (hard to think), headaches, snoring and 'crankiness'. If you suffer sinus problems all the time, it may be useful to watch your diet. Foods which often seem to be a problem include wine, dairy products, brewed drinks and monosodium glutamate.

Herbs that help include horehound, garlic, fenugreek, mullein—all herbs that help remove congestion.

Essential oils in steam are excellent here. Boil a few litres of water, put this into a shallow bowl with a few drops of The Fragrant Garden Breathe Easy Oil, eucalyptus oil or thyme oil. Put a towel over your head and breathe in the medicated vapours for about half an hour. Keep blowing your nose to help get rid of the mucus. Don't worry if this treatment seems to make things worse by creating lots of mucus. In fact, the mucus has been dislodged by the steam and essential oil.

Try to avoid milk products and alcohol for a while and see if this helps. A few drops of The Fragrant Garden Breathe Easy Oil on the pillow at night is helpful for congestion. Horseradish is also an extremely useful vegetable to aid in easing sinusitis. Beta-carotene (the precursor of vitamin A) is excellent for many. Take one or two capsules for seven to ten days.

Skin Rashes

There are dozens of herbs used for skin problems, just as there are dozens of different kinds and causes of skin problems. Different herbs help different rashes and different people. Most herbalists believe that a rash is a symptom of an internal complaint and prescribe 'blood cleansing' herbs or diet. Nutritional supplements such as zinc, vitamins B_6 and E can help.

Before you rush off to seek professional advice, try these herbs:

Comfrey

Comfrey is available as an ointment or cream, or you can make a strong decoction (i.e. a tea boiled rather than infused) of the roots and leaves. Wash the roots with a nail brush before boiling. Decoctions can be added to the bath (use one or two cups) or can be applied directly to the rash. Comfrey-infused oil can be made by soaking diced root with an equal quantity of olive oil. Leave this in a warm spot for a week, then use as you would a cream. It is a good idea to add a little lavender or rosemary essential oil to your comfrey oil too (up to 2 ml in 100 ml).

Aloe vera

Where possible use the fresh gel from either the Indian aloe or the large true aloe. The leaves should be at least 2.5–5 cm wide at the base. Younger leaves are less effective. The yellow sap works well too, but it stains.

Camomile

Camomile is an anti-inflammatory herb. Use a little of the essential oil mixed in with your comfrey ointment or make a strong tea of the flowers. Add it to a bath along with some honeysuckle and soak in it. Six to ten drops of The Fragrant Garden Camomile Oil can be added to the bath nightly.

Honeysuckle

An old Chinese remedy is to boil the fresh leaves, cool, then apply the decoction or soak in a bath to which it has been added. We had a customer succeed with this when all else had failed.

Golden Seal

Golden Seal *(Hydrastis canadensis)* is an American Indian herb available as an ointment that is sometimes effective on the most stubborn of rashes.

Olive Oil

Rub a little on the rash. This is good for dry, flaky rashes. Try also taking by mouth (a dessertspoonful a day), perhaps with a little lemon juice.

Tea Tree Essential Oil

Try using three to nine drops a day if you suspect a fungal problem.

Vitamin E Oil

Use the oil direct or add it to comfrey ointment. It seems to be very soothing for many skin problems.

Lavender Essential Oil

Add three to nine drops to the bath nightly.

Chickweed *(Stellaria media)*

This can be a very soothing herb for eczema. Use as ointment or oil.

The 'Grand Cure'

You can adapt this recipe by using fresh or store-bought herbs or by adding or subtracting for your own brews. Place in blender:

> 100 ml sorbolene
> A good dash of virgin olive oil
> A small jar of comfrey ointment
> A small jar of Golden Seal ointment
> The contents of a few Vitamin E capsules
> The gel from a fresh Aloe vera leaf
> 10 to 20 drops of your favourite essential oil (lavender perhaps)

Blend until well mixed. Store in the refrigerator and use as necessary. It will keep for about two weeks.

Sleep Herbs

(See also Calming Herbs in Arthritis Section)

In a very old undated medical book of mine, William Whitla M.D., 'Professor of Therapeutics in Queen's College, Belfast' gives this obviously Irish remedy:

> Of the drugs used to counteract sleeplessness, there is not, on the whole, one so generally valuable as Alcohol in most mild cases. The various wines are inferior to whisky, and brandy does not produce as good results as whisky. Strong ale is highly hypnotic, and so is porter or stout. Alcohol acts more certainly if given warm, but not hot. One wine-glassful of good whisky, made into warm punch, and swallowed as a draught—not sipped in spoonfuls—is a most invaluable soporific.[92]

It should be noted that alcohol can also act as a stimulant and keep you awake or wake you up in the wee small hours.

Two herbs that are very effective calm-me-downs are passionfruit flowers and valerian root. They are most effective as teas. (The tablets and tinctures of valerian do not seem to be as effective as a tea made from the dried roots. The parts of valerian that help sleep are volatile and unstable and are sometimes wholly or partly lost in manufacture or processing. Alcoholic tinctures are okay if they are freshly made.)

Take a cup of valerian and/or passionflower tea half an hour before bed. It is important to get reasonably fresh tea or store it in a well sealed jar. Valerian smells awful to many people, but fortunately it does not taste as bad as it smells. (The old chemists used to remove the smell from their hands by rubbing with sodium bicarbonate.)

Camomile tea is also a good calming herb, though not as strong as valerian. Camomile can be used with safety by very young children. Hop flowers are also very calming. They can be made into a tea, drunk as beer or just stuffed into a large pillow or left in a bowl in the bedroom.

Catnip *(Nepeta cataria)* is a gentle, relaxing herb. It is traditionally given to children boiled with sugar to make a syrup.

A few drops of lavender oil in the bath is relaxing.

Another simple remedy is to take a large dessertspoonful of honey, a pinch of cinnamon and a cup of warm milk. This works well with those people who eat early and then stay up late without eating in between.[93]

Tryptophan is a calming amino acid found in most plants. Evening primrose seeds have the highest amount of tryptophan, according to James Duke,[94] but the seeds need to be ground or they pass through the digestive system whole.

Do avoid substances that keep you awake. These include coffee, green or black (camellia) tea, Yerba maté, chocolate, cocoa, cola drinks and ginseng if taken with drinks containing caffeine. Some people find they can't drink these closer than 12 hours before bedtime! Avoid taking

vitamin tablets at night, especially strong multi-B tablets, as these can keep some people awake.

Sometimes, drugs such as cortisone can disturb sleep patterns. If all else fails, discuss your problems with a naturopath as there are other herbs, diet and lifestyle factors that may help.

Smoking (quitting)

> To cease smoking is the easiest thing I ever did; I ought to know because I've done it a thousand times.
>
> Mark Twain

Giving up smoking was one of the hardest things I ever did. It is also the best thing we can do for our bodies. After many stops and starts, two things finally helped me: Quincy and ginseng. 'Quincy'?—the old TV series! In one episode, the county coroner had a case of a baffling child poisoning. The child lay in the hospital dramatically dying from some mysterious, unknown poison. New to parenthood, I sat on the edge of my seat. At the stroke of doom the mystery poison was discovered—cigarette butts! The concentrated nicotine in the filters is deadly. I knew of nicotine's effectiveness in killing bugs in the garden— so with this motivation the pipe was thrown into the rubbish bin.

I found that over the next few months, strong ginseng tea (3–6 mg of ginseng to a cup, with honey) helped reduce the craving for tobacco. Ginseng is an excellent Chinese tonic herb. It stimulates the adrenal glands and gives you a 'lift'.

Ginseng tea is usually drunk weak and is quite pleasant. Strong ginseng tea tastes like boiled mud!

> The root of Ginseng is chewed as a substitute for tobacco. The juice should be swallowed.[95]

Roots of ginseng can be purchased and this might be an even better remedy than my tea. Guy, a local chef, who was always searching out arcane herbs and flavours, once gave me a taste of a ginseng brandy. The bottle had a whole ginseng root in it and had cost him a week's salary in Hong Kong. It tasted like a combination of methylated spirits and rocket fuel. No wonder most people prefer conventional medicine!

There are a number of other herbs that some people have found effective. I list them here for you to try:
• Carrots taken as necessary. Stop before you turn yellow!

- An alcoholic extract of fresh oats may be helpful.
- Lobelia *(Lobelia inflata)* contains lobeline, a chemical that affects the body in the same way as nicotine. It is not as addictive as nicotine. Lobelia can be taken as a tea or as anti-smoking lozenges and chewing gums. I am not keen on lobelia as it gives the same 'fix' as tobacco and so perpetuates the psychological dependence. Lobelia, however, is a very pretty herb to grow in a boggy spot in your garden.
- Chew on raw and unhulled sunflower seeds.
- Ginseng cigarettes seem to be available only in China. A friend found these cigarettes very effective while travelling in China. Ginseng is very difficult to grow in most of mainland Australia, but can be purchased as instant tea or tablets from health food shops. The tea is the most economical way of buying it. Try a cup every time you have the urge to smoke.

People with allergies will find giving up smoking more difficult than most. This is because smoking helps to mask allergies.

Snoring

He drank the Night away...
Then snor'd out all the Day

Oxford English Dictionary (1746)

Place a few drops of The Fragrant Garden Breathe Easy Oil on the pillow at night, on a light ring or in a scent pot in the room overnight. The Fragrant Garden Breathe Easy Pot Pourri is also helpful. Put some in a large bowl in the bedroom and refresh with a drop of the oil nightly.

Often snoring is caused by congested airways, especially the sinuses. A change in diet, avoiding alcohol and/or beef, milk and cheese can be helpful. One of my female customers once said 'Why do men always snore when they drink?' While this is a physical impossibility, alcohol may make one snore more at night due to its depressant effect on muscles of the upper airways, causing some degree of obstruction. Unfortunately, there is only one way to find out if this is the cause of your snoring problems. Stop drinking!

Some naturopaths suggest you avoid foods that they feel create mucus, such as refined carbohydrates and dairy products.

See also the section on sinus as snoring can be caused by congested sinuses.

Sore Throat

For those who have to clear their throats so often during a talk there is a simple, inexpensive, harmless effective remedy: Cloves—try it ... Just before going on the radio, or just before beginning a public talk, put two or three cloves in the mouth and chew and swallow slowly. That is all.[96]

Here is my famous, not-yet-patented cure.

Take a sprig of fresh sage, six sprigs of fresh lemon thyme, a sprig of yarrow and a comfrey leaf. Place in two cups of water and bring to the boil. Sweeten with a little honey and sip this tea throughout the day. Sage is astringent and antiseptic, thyme is antiseptic, comfrey is soothing and healing, yarrow is a very old herb (it reduces temperature and is anti-inflammatory) and I like to include it. This can really help if you take it before the sore throat fully develops. It is best drunk warm to hot as hot drinks are also efficacious for sore throats.

> Thyme makes matter out of ye Thorax, easy to come up.
>
> Dioscorides

A piece of clear, fresh aloe gel placed between the teeth and cheek and slowly sucked is also helpful. Try not to get any of the yellow sap as it is incredibly bitter. The yellow sap is healing too, but it tastes just awful. Wash it off the clear inner gel before using.

The Chinese use a decoction (strongly boiled-up tea) of honeysuckle flowers with a little natural liquorice. Gargling with this helps laryngitis. Honeysuckle is a climber which grows wild everywhere. It has gold and white fragrant flowers.

> Slippery Elm boiled in water makes one of the best gargles for a sore throat that can be supplied by the whole list of medicines. It should be sweetened with sugar.[97]

If you don't have these herbs on hand, use a teaspoon of salt in a glass of water (as hot as you can stand) and gargle for about three minutes. Do not swallow. Salty water is a strong disinfectant.

Sunburn
(See also Burns)

Sunburn should be prevented with lots of fresh sunscreen lotion put on half an hour before going out into the sun. The sunscreen should then be reapplied every hour if you have been swimming, or every two hours if you are not wet.

The best herb for sunburn is Aloe vera gel/juice. Our two-year-old daughter spent the day in a backyard pool with some bronzed Italian friends. She came home raspberry red all over, much to everyone's horror. The poor little girl was in terrible pain. We slathered her all over with fresh aloe gel from the garden. After the second application her pain was virtually gone. Without aloe she would not have been able to sleep. The next morning she had all but recovered and there was no blistering. This was interesting because she is a redhead with very fair skin.

A long soak in the bath with two to three drops of essential oil of lavender and two to three of camomile oil added to the water is also soothing. (Do not use craft perfume oils, only good-quality medicinal oils.) Blend a large, peeled aloe leaf and add this to the water also.

Quite a few medications (such as Largactil) and even one or two herbs (such as untreated bergamot orange oil, often used in Eau de Cologne) can cause increased sensitivity to the sun's rays and thus cause more burning. Most bergamot oils now have the offending, skin-sensitising chemical removed from them. Most colognes are now made with synthetic bergamot because of the high price of the natural oil, but if you do use colognes and you do burn, perhaps you should check your brand.

Sunspots

It's a good idea always to have any unusual skin lumps and bumps and discolourations checked out by your doctor. In the meantime, try comfrey ointment or fresh Aloe vera gel daily. Comfrey is amazing. I have seen many people clear up a whole range of very nasty skin problems with four to six weeks of religious application of comfrey ointment or cream. Prevention is the best cure. Always wear a hat and lots of fresh sunscreen when outdoors.

Sweating Too Much

Horses sweat. Ladies perspire.

Mary Evans, Jan's maternal grandmother, quoting
a long line of Victorian ladies

Sage is the classic drying herb for those who feel they are perspiring too much. Place a sprig of fresh sage in a cup of hot water, sweeten to taste and sip. Take as necessary. A drop or two of essential oil of sage can also be used as an underarm deodorant.

Teeth

Rub a fresh sage leaf on your teeth for whiter, cleaner teeth. It is quite amazing how sage leaves do remove plaque. Even if you think your teeth are clean, take a fresh sage leaf and rub it over your teeth. You can see the plaque collect on the leaf!

Toothache

A drop of essential oil of clove or cinnamon will temporarily numb the pain of a toothache. The oil acts like a local anaesthetic. Essential oils are strong bactericides. Clove oil is still used by dentists for this reason. As this is an unpleasant remedy for children, use very small amounts or try lime essential oil, which is not quite so irritating. You can use a very small amount of oil by dipping a toothpick in the oil and placing this on the offending tooth. The toothpick also helps you place the oil in exactly the right spot. This is, of course, only first aid and you should see your dentist as soon as possible.

Try chewing catmint *(Nepeta cataria)* leaves. This is an old remedy. A Chinese remedy is to chew a piece of ginger root.

Some herbalists suggest that the juice and rind of a lemon is useful not only for brushing teeth and gums, where it kills bacteria, but when mixed with saliva and chewed slowly, it helps remove plaque and tartar from the surface of the teeth. Barbara Griggs also mentions the use of lemon in this way, but feels the acid might damage the enamel.[98]

Tooth decay

Drinks containing tannins, such as tea and coffee, interfere with the bacterial processes leading to tooth decay. Most astringent herbs contain tannins. Tannin curdles protein and has been used to tan animal hides.

Thrush—see Candida

Tinea—see Athlete's Foot

Tummy

The stomach is the house of disease, and diet is the head of healing, for the origin of all sickness is indigestion.

Tawaddud in *The Arabian Nights*, c.850 AD

The classic tummy herbs are peppermint and camomile. Camomile has been shown to have a dramatic antispasmodic (calming and settling) effect on the stomach.[99] Try a cup of herb tea containing both camomile and peppermint.

For more severe cases try Golden Seal tablets, tincture or tea. The tea is possibly the most effective but it's probably the worst thing you have ever tasted.

Mucilaginous herbs such as slippery elm powder, comfrey and Aloe vera gel are helpful. As they put a soothing lining on the wall of the stomach they are good for ulcers and acidity problems. Peel the aloe, remove all the yellow sap which is very bitter, blend with fruit juice, hold your nose and drink. Comfrey can be made into a tea, or the leaves can be juiced. Use in moderation as very large amounts of comfrey taken over a long period may cause a build-up of liver toxins. Give your system a break from comfrey occasionally.

Ulcers

Leg

We had a young woman call on us early one spring to buy a dozen comfrey plants. As it was early in spring we just found a dozen. Comfrey usually goes underground for our mild winters. A week later the woman rang asking us to freight her another dozen, as quickly as possible. She came the following week for twenty more plants. As comfrey is the fastest growing plant and one plant is usually adequate for most people, our curiosity was aroused. It turned out that her mother had had a leg ulcer for many years. Finally, it had become so bad that her doctor had recommended she have her leg amputated. At this, her daughter had contacted an old herbalist who told her to make comfrey root poultices for the ulcer. This she was doing every day, and was therefore using an incredible number of comfrey plants. This is an old remedy little used today because it is unaesthetic, time consuming to prepare and messy. It involves harvesting, cleaning and mashing the root, applying it to the ulcer and tying it on with bandages. We sent the woman off to an organic farming friend who had comfrey taking over her garden and was only too happy to have someone 'weed' it for her.

A few months later she wandered into the nursery and told us that her mother's leg was completely cured.

Comfrey ointment can be used in place of poultices, although a fresh plant poultice always heals more quickly. Apply the ointment liberally once or twice a day to the edges of the ulcer, working from the good skin to the bad. Comfrey promotes the growth of healthy tissue.

Stomach

Liquorice *(Glycyrrhiza glabra)* is excellent for peptic and gastric ulcers. Don't eat the lolly as most liquorice lollies are made with synthetic anise flavour. You can buy a solid extract imported from Italy. Eat about ¼ teaspoon of this before meals. Liquorice should not be taken to excess by people with high blood pressure, kidney disease or those taking heart medicine. If in doubt, discuss with your naturopath. Both olive oil and raw cabbage juice have been used for ulcers, so include some in your diet. Wherever possible, olive oil should be taken uncooked. Extra virgin olive oil is perhaps the best and has a wonderful flavour.

Fenugreek *(Trigonella foenum-graecum)* seed tea is a Chinese folk remedy for peptic ulcers which modern research has shown to be effective.

Mouth

Myrrh tincture used as a mouthwash is an effective antiseptic. It tastes terrible, but it works!

Warts

Warts can be removed by the sap of a number of herbs. Greater celandine, dandelion or Petty spurge are all useful. Be careful that the juice is only applied to the wart, not the surrounding skin. Dandelion seems most effective in spring. This is because there are different chemicals in the plant at this time of the year. Break off a flower or a seed head and put the white sap from the stem on the wart. Do this until the wart disappears. Our daughter, Elizabeth, had a wart and we tried this remedy several times in late winter without much success. In early spring, we put the white sap from a big, fat, juicy dandelion on the wart and the next day the wart started to go black. Within a week it was gone.

Greater celandine is used in the same way. The yellow juice from the leaves is painted onto the warts daily, with special attention to the first wart that appeared. Celandine can be used any time, although the old herbals say it should be gathered when 'the Sun is in Leo and the moon in Aries'.

Petty Spurge can also be used. Dab the white milky substance from the broken stem on the wart two or three times daily for two to three weeks or until the wart disappears.

For these remedies to be successful, they must be used consistently.

Worms

Worms are parasites that live in the bowel. There are various types—tapeworms, roundworms, threadworms and hookworms. The most common found in human beings is the tiny threadworm, which settles in the intestines and multiplies by crawling out to lay its eggs around the anus—usually at night. The worms look like tiny threads of fine cotton, dirty white in colour, and can be seen around a child's anus when the child is asleep. Often children pick worms up by playing in dirt or with animal faeces, or by not washing their hands. They can then pass them on to the rest of the family. Children often get very cranky and irritable when they have worms. Most of the traditional European remedies for worms (such as wormwood) might be a little on the bitter side and can be toxic if taken to excess. It is probably best, then, that you seek professional help if you want to eradicate worms herbally.

There are a number of foods that are said to discourage worms. These include coconut, garlic, onions, paw paw, pomegranates, pumpkin seeds, cabbage, horseradish, figs and pineapple. Certainly, a whole garlic clove in a dog's daily diet seems to keep them worm-free. Old chook fanciers did the same thing, but crushed the garlic through the hen mash.

A traditional Chinese remedy for tapeworm involves eating a whole coconut and drinking its milk first thing in the morning for three days. Green paw paw is also used in China for tapeworm, roundworm, whipworm and other intestinal parasites. The flesh of unripe young paw paws is sliced and soaked for some time in vinegar; 250 g of this, along with 60 ml of the vinegar, is taken each evening before going to bed. Do this for three days.[100]

A diet low in refined sugars is said to be helpful.

Wrinkles

Wrinkles should merely indicate where smiles have been.

Mark Twain

Comfrey and Aloe vera both contain the chemical allantoin—found in only the best and dearest anti-wrinkle creams! You can grow your own fresh aloe and buy comfrey cream or ointment at any health food shop. A good quality comfrey cream regularly applied is great for wrinkles and skin generally.

If you have oily skin use fresh aloe gel straight from the plant. If your skin is on the dry side, use some moisturiser with it as aloe is astringent and can be drying.

Nothing has ever given me greater pleasure than herbs. It was my father who first taught me the magic of plants that grow in the earth. And I have amassed a great volume of experience for myself in my long years of dealing with herbs. It is only right that I should share that experience with everybody. I hope that by writing this book I am leaving a message to future generations. Let us hope that the destruction and pollution that our civilisation wreaks upon nature will be brought to a halt; let us hope that our children in their turn will have the chance to admire the cornflower and the poppy and the wild rose and rejoice in their beauty ... before they use them to ease their complaints.

Maurice Mességué 1975[101]

If you have a favourite old-time practical recipe for using plants or essential oils that you would like to pass on to future generations, drop me a line, giving as much detail as you can. Tell of any personal use you have of the remedy. I would be very grateful.

M.V.B.

References

1. E.J. Pizzorno and M.T. Murray, *A Textbook of Natural Medicine*, John Bastyr College Publications, Washington, 1987.
2. Dr P.M. Kidd, 'Germanium-132 Haemostatic Normaliser and Immunostimulant. A review of its preventative and therapeutic efficacy', *International Clinical Nutrition Review*, Vol 7, No 1, January 1987.
3. R. Buist, *Food Intolerance*, Harper Row, Sydney, 1984.
4. R. Buist, *Food Chemical Sensitivity*, Harper Row, Sydney, 1986.
5. *The Lawrence Review of Natural Products*, Pharmaceutical Associates, Pennsylvania.
6. *The Herbalist*, Research Vol 2, No 2, 1989, p.18.
7. Simon Mills, *Dictionary of Modern Herbalism*, Lothian, Melbourne, 1981.
8. Anon.
9. Pizzorno and Murray, *A Textbook of Natural Medicine*, p.218, 353.
10. Pizzorno and Murray, *A Textbook of Natural Medicine*, p.116.
11. W. Whitla, *A Dictionary of Treatment or Therapeutic Index including Medical and Surgical Therapeutics*, London.
12. S.W. Woolley and G.P. Forrester, *Pharmaceutical Formulas*, 10th ed., The Chemical and Druggist, London, 1929.
13. L. Inaba and Y. Inaba, 'Male Pattern Baldness: Sebaceous Gland Hypothesis' in *Cosmetics & Toiletries*, July 1990.
14. J. Wilen and L. Wilen, *Chicken Soup and Other Folk Remedies*, Fawcett Columbine, New York, 1984.
15. J. Carper, *The Food Pharmacy*, Bantam, New York, 1988, pp.246-50.
16. C.F. Leyel, *Green Medicine*, Faber & Faber, London.
17. G. Firth, *Secrets of the Still*, EPM Publications, Virginia, 1983.
18. M.T. Quelch, *Herbs for Daily Use*, Faber, London, 1941, p.74.
19. N. Culpeper, *Culpeper's English Family Physician*, W. Locke, UK, 1792.
20. Quelch, *Herbs for Daily Use*, p.98.
21. Quelch, *Herbs for Daily Use*, p.98.
22. Prof. M. Kearney, in an address to Natural Products Seminar, University of New South Wales, 1989.
23. Kidd, 'Germanium-132 Haemostatic Normaliser and Immunostimulant'.
24. Kidd, 'Germanium-132 Haemostatic Normaliser and Immunostimulant'.
25. G. Vines, *New Scientist*, 9 July, 1994, pp.14-15.
26. M. Mességué, *Health Secrets of Plants and Herbs*, Pan, UK, 1981, p.288.

27. M. Grieve, *A Modern Herbal*, Dover, New York, (1931) 1971, p.839.
28. Grieve, *A Modern Herbal*, p.839.
29. Culpeper, *Culpeper's English Family Physician*.
30. N. Coon, *The Complete Book of Violets*, Barnes & Co., New Jersey, 1977, p.30.
31. Dr J.L. Hartwell, National Cancer Institute, USA, quoted in N. Coon, *The Complete Book of Violets*, p.81.
32. M. Lipkin, quoted in the *The Natural Healing and Nutrition Annual*, Rodale Press, 1988, p.26.
33. *Archives of International Medicine*, 1980.
34. R. Burton, quoted in the *Dictionary of Quotations*, Penguin, London, 1960.
35. Carper, *The Food Pharmacy*, p.189.
36. Professor V.E. Tyler, Some Potentially Useful Drugs Identified in a Study of Folk Medicine, in *Proceedings of The First National Herb Growing and Marketing Conference*, Purdue University, Indiana, 1986.
37. *The Lawrence Review of Natural Products*, Pharmaceutical Associates.
38. Phelan and Juardo, *Journal of Surgery*, 1963.
39. Carper, *The Food Pharmacy*, p.250.
40. A.Y. Leung, *Chinese Herbal Remedies*, Universe Books, New York, 1984, p.125.
41. Y. Dai and C. Lui, *Fruit as Medicine*, The Ram's Skull Press, Australia, 1986, p.101.
42. P. Logan, *Irish Country Cure*, Appletree Press, North Ireland, 1981.
43. Dioscorides, in Gunther, R.T. (ed.) *The Greek Herbal of Dioscorides*, Hafner Reprint, New York, 1968.
44. *The Lawrence Review of Natural Products*, Pharmaceutical Associates.
45. *The Lawrence Review of Natural Products*, Pharmaceutical Associates.
46. Carper, *The Food Pharmacy*, pp.207–10.
47. Leung, *Chinese Herbal Remedies*, p.72.
48. Leung, *Chinese Herbal Remedies*, p.91.
49. J. Gerard, *The Herbal or General History of Plants*, Dover, New York, (1633) 1975, p.1302.
50. Carper, *The Food Pharmacy*, pp.246–8.
51. P. Hauseman and J. Hurley, *The Healing Foods*, Rodale Press, Pennsylvania, 1989, p.140.
52. *The Lawrence Review of Natural Products*, Pharmaceutical Associates.
53. Pizzorno and Murray, *Encyclopedia of Natural Medicine*, Macmillan, Washington, 1990.
54. Leung, *Chinese Herbal Remedies*, p.133.
55. J. Kloss, *Back to Eden*, Lifeline Books, California, (1939), 1972p.
56. H. Ward, *Herbal Manual*, Fowler, London, 1983, p.121.
57. Pizzorno and Murray, *Encyclopedia of Natural Medicine*, p.360.
58. Leung, *Chinese Herbal Remedies*, p.70.
59. D. Law, *Herb Growing for Health*, Arco, New York, 1969.
60. Wilen and Wilen, *Chicken Soup and Other Folk Remedies*.
61. Wilen and Wilen, *Chicken Soup and Other Folk Remedies*, p.81.
62. Leung, *Chinese Herbal Remedies*, p.133.
63. Carper, *The Food Pharmacy*, pp.143–5.
64. Meyer, *The Herbalist*.

65. C. Nemeroff, 'MSG Induced Neurotoxicity' in Miller, S.A. *Nutrition and Behaviour*, Franklin Institute Press, Williamsburg, 1981.
66. Pizzorno and Murray, *Encyclopedia of Natural Medicine*, pp.311, 330.
67. Pizzorno and Murray, *Encyclopedia of Natural Medicine*, p.330.
68. Pizzorno and Murray, *A Textbook of Natural Medicine*, p.30.
69. S. Kirchheimer and the Editors of Prevention magazine, *The Doctor's Book of Home Remedies II*, Rodale Press, Pennsylvania, 1993.
70. Hauseman and Hurley, *The Healing Foods*.
71. Leung, *Chinese Herbal Remedies*, p.86.
72. Wilen and Wilen, *Chicken Soup and Other Folk Remedies*, p.96.
73. D. Law, *Herb Growing for Health*.
74. Alexis, quoted in Leyel, *Green Medicine*, Faber and Faber, London.
75. H. Wagner, 'Immunostimulants from Medicinal Plants' in *Advances in Chinese Medicinal Materials Research*, World Scientific Publishing Co., Singapore, 1985.
76. Prof. V.E. Tyler, 'Some Potentially Useful Drugs Identified in a Study of Folk Medicine', p.44.
77. W. Whitla, *A Dictionary of Treatment*.
78. Wilen and Wilen, *Chicken Soup and Other Folk Remedies*.
79. Florsheim et al., *Schweiz Med Wochen*, Vol 112, Germany, 1982.
80. *The Lawrence Review of Natural Products*, Pharmaceutical Associates.
81. Leung, *Chinese Herbal Remedies*, p.79.
82. S. Fulder, *The Root of Being*, Hutchinson, Essex, 1980, p.298.
83. L. Hay, *You Can Heal Your Life*, Specialist Publications, Concord, Australia, 1988.
84. R. Walford, *Maximum Life Span*, W.W. Norton & Co., New York, 1983, chapter 5.
85. R. Pelton, *Mind Food & Smart Pills*, Doubleday, New York, 1989, p.169.
86. D. Waters of Pennyroyal Herb Farm, Australia, personal communication.
87. D. Hoffman, *The Herbal Handbook*, Healing Arts Press, Vermont, 1987, p.147.
88. J. Duke, *Handbook of Edible Weeds*, CRC Press, Florida, 1992.
89. J. Gerard, *The Herbal or General History of Plants*, 1633, Dover, New York, 1975.
90. Lewis and Lewis, *Medical Botany*, John Wiley, New York, 1977.
91. Leung, *Chinese Herbal Remedies*, p.164.
92. W. Whitla, *A Dictionary of Treatment*.
93. Pizzorno and Murray, *Encyclopedia of Natural Medicine*, p.392.
94. J. Duke, *Handbook of Edible Weeds*.
95. J. Meyer, *The Herbalist*.
96. D. Meyer and C. Meyer, *The Herbalist Almanac, A 50-Year Anthology*, Meyerbooks, Illinois, p.250.
97. Hills Family Herbal, quoted in D. Meyer and C. Meyer, *The Herbalist Almanac*, p.139.
98. B. Griggs, *The Green Witch—A Modern Woman's Herbal*, Vermilion, 1994.
99. Forrestrer, *Planta Medica*, Vol 40, 1980.
100. Dai and Cheng, *Fruit as Medicine*, pp.90–1.
101. Messague, *Health Secrets of Plants and Herbs*, p.6.

Bibliography

Blackall, Simon 1989, *Food for Thought*, Watermark Press, Surry Hills.

Bricklin, Mark (ed.) 1982, *Rodale's Encyclopedia of Natural Home Remedies*, Rodale Press, Pennsylvania.

Bricklin, Mark 1988, *The Natural Healing and Nutrition Annual*, Rodale, Pennsylvania.

Buist, Robert 1984, *Food Intolerance*, Harper Row, Sydney.

Buist, Robert 1986, *Food Chemical Sensitivity*, Harper Row, Sydney.

Burton, Robert 1960, in *The Dictionary of Quotations*, Penguin, London.

Carper, Jean 1988, *The Food Pharmacy*, Bantam, New York.

Chang, Yeung, Tso, and Koo 1985, *Advances in Chinese Medicinal Materials Research*, World Scientific Publishing Co., Singapore.

Cohen, J.M. & M.J. 1991, *The Penguin Dictionary of Quotations*, Bloomsbury Books, London.

Coon Nelson, A.S. 1977, *The Complete Book of Violets*, Barnes & Co., New Jersey.

Culpeper, N. 1792, *Culpeper's English Family Physician or Medical Herbal Enlarged*, Vol. 1, W. Locke, London.

Dai Yin-fang & Lui Cheng-Jun 1986, *Fruit as Medicine*, The Ram's Skull Press, Kuranda, Australia.

Duke, James 1992, *Handbook of Edible Weeds*, CRC Press, Florida.

Eco, Umberto 1984, *The Name of the Rose*, Pan, London.

Firth, Grace 1983, *Secrets of the Still*, EPM Publications, Virginia.

Florsheim et. al. 1982, *Schweiz Med Wochen*, Vol 112, Germany.

Forrester, G.P. 1934, *The Chemist's Recipe Book*, The Chemist and Druggist, London.

Forrestrer 1980, *Planta Medica*, Vol 40.

Fulder, Stephen 1980, *The Root of Being*, Hutchinson, Essex.

Geràrd, John 1975, *The Herbal or General History of Plants*, 1633, Dover, New York.

Gorman, James 1982, *First Aid for Hypochiandriacs*, Workman, New York.

Grieve, Mrs M. 1971, *A Modern Herbal*, Dover, New York.

Griggs, Barbara 1991, *The Green Witch—A Modern Woman's Herbal*, Vermilion.

Gunther, Robert T. (ed.) 1968, *The Greek Herbal of Dioscorides, illustrated by a Byzantine A.D. 512, Englished by John Goodyear A.D. 1655*, Hafner Reprint, New York.

P. Hauseman and J.B. Hurley 1989, *The Healing Foods*, Rodale Press, Pennsylvania.

Hay, Louise 1988, *You Can Heal Your Life*, Specialist Publications, Concord, Australia.

Hill, John 1756, *The British Herbal, an History of Plants and Trees*, Osborne & J. Shipton, London.

Hills, Lawrence, *Comfrey, Past, Present and Future*, Faber and Faber, London.

Hiscox, Gardner (ed.) 1981, *Henley's Twentieth Century Book of Formulas, Processes and Trade Secrets*, Publishers' Agency, Pennsylvania.

Hoffman, David 1987, *The Herbal Handbook*, Healing Arts Press, Vermont.

Inaba & Inaba, Y. 1990, 'Male Pattern Baldness: Sebaceous Gland Hypothesis' in *Cosmetics & Toiletries*, July 1990.

Kidd, Dr Parris M. 1987, 'Germanium-132 Haemostatic Normaliser and Immunostimulant. A review of its preventative and therapeutic efficacy', in *International Clinical Review*, Vol 7, No 1, January 1987.

Kirchheimer and the Editors of Prevention Magazine Health Books 1983, *The Doctors Book of Home Remedies II*, Rodale Press, Pennsylvania.

Kloss, J. 1972, *Back to Eden*, Lifeline Books, California.

Law, Donald 1969, *Herb Growing for Health*, Arco, New York.

Leung, Albert Y. 1984, *Chinese Herbal Remedies*, Universe Books, New York.

Lewis and Lewis, Elvin 1977, *Medical Botany*, John Wiley, New York.

C.F. Leyel, *Green Medicine*, Faber & Faber, London.

Lipkin, M. 1988, quoted in *The Natural Healing and Nutrition Annual*, 1988, Rodale Press, Pennsylvania.

Logan, Patrick 1981, *Irish Country Cures*, Appletree Press, North Ireland.

Messague, Maurice 1981, *Health Secrets of Plants and Herbs*, Pan, UK.

Metcalf, Fred (Comp.) 1986, *The Penguin Dictionary of Modern Humorous Quotations*, Penguin, London.

Meyer, D. and Meyer, C. *The Herbalist Almanac*, A 50-Year Anthology, Meyerbooks, Illinois.

Meyer, Joseph E., *The Herbalist*, Meyerbooks, Illinois.

Meyer, Joseph E. 1988, *The Herbalist Almanac*, Meyerbooks, Illinois.

Mills, S. 1985, *Dictionary of Modern Herbalism*, Lothian, Melbourne.

Nemeroff, Charles 1981, 'MSG Induced Neurotoxicity' in Miller, Stanford A. 1981, *Nutrition & Behaviour*, Franklin Institute Press, Williamsburg.

Payer, Lynn 1988, *Medicine & Culture*, Henry Holt.

Pelton, Ross 1989, *Mind Food & Smart Pills*, Doubleday, New York.

Pizzorno, Joseph E. and Murray, Micheal T. 1987, *A Textbook of Natural Medicine*, John Bastyr College Publications, Washington.

Pizzorno, Joseph E. and Murray, Micheal T. 1990, *Encyclopedia of Natural Medicine*, Macmillan, Washington.

Pratchett, Terry 1981, *Strata*, Corgi, Great Britain.

Quelch, Mary Thorne 1981, *The Herb Garden*, Faber & Faber, London.

Quelch, Mary Thorne 1941, *Herbs for Daily Use*, Faber, London.

Rawson, Hugh and Millner, Margaret (eds) 1988, *The New International Dictionary of Quotations*, Signet, New York.

Rose, Jeanne 1985, *Herbs and Things*, Jeanne Rose's Herbal, Putnam, New York.

Sharpless, Stanley, J. 'Cupid's Nightcap', quoted in Miller, Stanford A. 1981, *Nutrition & Behaviour*, Franklin Institute Press, Williamsburg.

Spenser, Edmund, quoted in Telesco, Patricia 1993, *A Victorian Grimoire*, Llewellyn, St Paul.

Susumu, Hiai 1985, 'Chinese Medicinal Material and the Secretion of ACTH and Corticosteroid' in *Advances in Chinese Medicinal Materials Research*, World Scientific Publishing Co., Singapore.

Suzuki, David 1990, *Inventing the Future*, Allen & Unwin, Sydney.

The Lawrence Review of Natural Products, a monthly newsletter published by Pharmaceutical Information Associates, Pennsylvania.

Thompson, Samuel 1883, *New Guide to Health*, Jarvis Pike & Co., Ohio.

Tyler, Professor, V.E. 1986, 'Some Potentially Useful Drugs Identified in a Study of Folk Medicine' in *Proceedings of the First National Herb Growing and Marketing Conference*, Purdue University Press, Indiana.

Tyler, Varro E. 1985, *Hoosier Home Remedies*, Purdue University Press, Indiana.

Vines, Gail 1994, in *New Scientist* magazine, 9 July 1994.

Wagner, Hildert 1985, 'Immunostimulants from Medicinal Plants' in Advances in *Chinese Medicinal Research*, World Scientific Publishing Co., Singapore.

Walford, Ray 1983, *Maximum Life Span*, W.W. Norton & Company, New York.

Walford, Ray 1986, *The 120 Year Diet*, Simon & Schuster.

Ward, Harold 1983, *Herbal Manual*, Fowler, London.

Wheelright, Edith Grey 1974, *Medicinal Plants and Their History*, Dover.

Wilen, Joan and Wilen, Lydia 1984, *Chicken Soup and Other Folk Remedies*, Fawcett Columbine, New York.

Whitla, William, *A Dictionary of Treatment of Therapeutic Index including Medical and Surgical Therapeutics*, London.

Woolley, S.W. & Forester, G.P. 1929, *Pharmaceutical Formulas*, Vol 1, published at the offices of 'The Chemist and Druggist', London.

Worth, Valerie 1971, *The Crone's Book of Words*, Llewellyn, St Paul.

Index

Lavender essential oil *(Lavendula vera, angustifolia, officinalis)*, 5, 10, 20, 28-9, 32, 43, 57, 59, 63, 70, 74, 81, 85-6, 96, 99, 101, 105

Lemon *(Citrus limonum)*, 4, 25-6, 28, 35, 49, 59, 61-2, 68, 83, 106

Lemon Balm *(Melissa officinalis)*, 4, 65, 82

Lemon Thyme *(Thymus citriodorus)*, 4, 22, 50, 104

Lemon Verbena *(Aloysia triphylla)*, 65

Liquorice *(Glycyrrhiza glabra)*, 4, 20, 50, 55-6, 59, 62, 104, 109

Lobelia *(Lobelia inflata)*, 103

Marigold/calendula *(Calendula officinalis)*, 6, 45

Marijuana *(Cannabis sativa)*, 76, 95

Marshmallow *(Althera officinalis)*, 84

Meadowsweet *(Spiraea ulmaria)*, 4, 16, 20, 72, 77, 93

Metamucil, 54, 78

Milk, 40, 52, 70, 98, 101, 103

Milk Thistle *(Silybum marianum)*, 86-7

Mint *(Mentha)*, 4, 22, 45, 83, 85

Mistletoe *(Viscum album)*, 27

MSG, 73

Mugwort *(Anthemis vulgaria)*, 4, 70-2, 85

Muira-puama (Potency Wood) *(Muira-puama)*, 12

Mulberries *(Morus nigra)*, 61

Mullein *(Verbascum thapsus)*, 27, 97

Mustard *(Brassica* spp.*)*, 40

Mustard greens, 40

Myrrh *(Commiphora myrrha)*, 59, 109

Nutmeg *(Myristica fragrans)*, 65

Nutmeg essential oil *(Myristica fragrans)*, 64, 66

Oat bran/meal *(Avena sativa)*, 56, 65, 103

Olive leaves *(Olea europaea)*, 27

Olive oil *(Olea europaea)*, 49, 51, 56, 64, 69, 70, 96, 99, 100

Onions *(Allium* spp.*)*, 4, 27, 44, 56, 61-2, 83, 109

Orange blossom *(Citrus vulgaris)*, 96

Oranges *(Citrus vulgaris)*, 15, 56, 82-3

Parsley *(Carum petroselinum)*, 4, 22, 45

Passionfruit flowers *(Passiflora incarnata)*, 100

Pau d'arco *(Tabebuia heptaphylla)*, 9

Paw Paw *(Carica papaya)*, 56, 109

Paw Paw Green *(Carica papaya)*, 109

Peanuts *(Arachis hypogaea)*, 49

Peas *(Pisum sativum)*, 95

Pennyroyal oil *(Mentha pulegium)*, 83, 85

Peppermint *(Mentha piperita)*, 4-5, 20, 32, 40, 53, 72-3, 93, 107

Peppermint essential oil *(Mentha piperita)*, 22, 47, 49, 57, 71-2, 85

Perilla *(Perilla frutescens)*, 77

Periwinkle Greater *(Vinca major)*, 27

Peroxide (Hydrogen), 69

Petty Spurge *(Euphorbia peplus)*, 109

Pilewort *(Ranunculus ficaria)*, 78

Pine nuts *(Pinus koraaiensis)*, 61

Pineapple *(Ananas comosus)*, 56, 62, 83, 109

Plantain—Psyllium *(Plantago major)*, 26, 54, 60-1, 78-9, 84

Plums *(Prunus* spp.*)*, 61

Pokeroot—Inkweed *(Phytolacca decandra)*, 19, 84

Pomegranates *(Punica granatum)*, 109

Potato *(Solanum tuberosum)*, 15, 59

Prickly Ash *(Aralia spinosa)*, 58

Pumpkin seeds *(Cucurbita pepo)*, 109

Quassia *(Quassia amara)*, 13

Quince *(Cydonia* spp.*)*, 93

Raspberry leaf *(Rubus idaeus)*, 26, 92

Rhubarb *(Rheum rhaponticum)*, 60-1, 67

Rice *(Sorbus)*, 11, 52

Rose Geranium *(Pelargonium graveolens)*, 21, 33

Rosemary *(Rosmarinus officinalis)*, 4, 23, 27, 89

Rosemary essential oil, 5, 16, 44, 64, 81, 85

Rue *(Ruta graveolens)*, 75

Rum, 62

Saffron *(Crocus sativus)*, 65-6

Sage *(Salvia officinalis)*, 4, 62, 80, 87, 89, 90, 92, 104, 106
Sage Red *(Salvia officinalis)*, 87
Salt, 4
Sandalwood essential oil *(Santalum album)*, 5, 11, 63, 74
Saw Palmetto *(Serenoa repens, Serenoa serrulata)*, 12
Seafood, 56, 64, 84
Seaweed, 27, 40, 84
Self Heal *(Prunella vulgaris)*, 26
Senna tea *(Cassia acutifolia)*, 60-1
Sesame seeds *(Sesamum indicum)*, 3-4, 80
Shiitake mushrooms, 40, 56
Skullcap *(Scutellaria lateriflora)*, 20
Slippery Elm *(Ulmus fulva)*, 5, 20, 49, 51, 61, 67-8, 79, 107
Southernwood *(Artemesia abrotanum)*, 4, 23-4
Soya bean, 37, 95
Spearmint *(Mentha viridus)*, 71
Spells, 45-6, 88
St. Mary's Thistle *(Carduus marianus)*, 79, 81
Strawberries *(Fragaria vesca)*, 15, 56, 77, 81-2
Sunflower seeds *(Helianthus annuus)*, 103
Swede, 40, 61
Sweet almond oil *(Amygdalus communis)*, 40
Sweet potatoes *(Ipomoea batatas)*, 40, 95

Tea *(Thea sinensis)*, 42, 62, 79, 107
Tea black *(Thea sinensis)*, 4-5, 101
Tea green *(Thea sinensis)*, 4-5, 27, 101
Tea Tree, 5, 72

Tea Tree essential oil *(Melaleuca alternifolia)*, 5, 22, 42, 59, 69, 74, 85-6, 96, 99
Thyme *(Thymus vulgaris)*, 3, 62, 104
Thyme essential oil *(Thymus vulgaris)*, 44, 97
Tobacco *(Nicotiana tabacum)*, 39
True Unicorn root *(Aletris farinosa)*, 94
Turmeric *(Curcuma longa)*, 95
Turnip *(Brassica campestris)*, 40
Turpentine, 61

Valerian *(Valeriana officinalis)*, 20, 35, 100
Violet *(Viola odorata)*, 17, 31, 37-8
Vitamin A, 98
Vitamin B, 3, 57, 65-6, 79, 80-1, 102
Vitamin C, 18, 57, 67, 76, 79
Vitamin E oil, 18, 51, 57, 79, 99
Vodka, 82

Water, 52
Watermelon *(Citrullus lanatus)*, 40
Wheat, 74
Whisky, 12, 100
White Willow *(Salix alba)*, 72, 82, 93
Wintergreen *(Gaultheria procumbens)*, 16, 61
Wood Betony *(Betonica officinalis)*, 4, 52-3
Wormwood *(Artemesia absinthium)*, 109

Yams *(Dioscorea* spp.), 95
Yarrow *(Achillea millefolium)*, 26, 46, 53, 71, 78, 104
Yerba Maté *(Illex paraguariensis)*, 79, 101
Yoghurt, 27, 40, 43, 56, 59
Yohimbe *(Pausinystalia yohimbe)*, 12

Zinc, 11, 64